THE ASTRAL PLANE

THE ASTRAL PLANE

C.W. LEADBEATER

Theosophical Manuals, No. 5

The Astral Plane: Its Scenery, Inhabitants, & Phenomena

Originally published in 1895
London: Theosophical Publishing Society
Benares: Theosophical Publishing Society
Madras: The Theosophist Office, Adyar

ISBN: 978-1-964003-19-1
First Printing, 2024

To Oliver
Happy Travels!

Contents

An Unexpected Journey

When I first stumbled upon the concept of astral projection, I wasn't deliberately seeking anything spiritual, mystical or transformative. At the time, I was a college student engaged in pretty normal experimentation and having the occasional existential crisis. I was often half-distracted by my classes, early-morning lectures, and late-night movies. My "Eureka" moment wasn't inspired by a guru's wisdom or a celestial visitation—it happened, rather unglamorously, in my dorm room after I'd pulled an all-nighter, half-awake and convinced I was dreaming. Except it wasn't a dream.

I felt a strange lightness, as though my body had become irrelevant, and I floated—effortlessly, inexplicably—far above myself. To say it was disorienting would be an understatement. I wasn't sure if I was still tethered to reality or if my mind had simply begun to unravel. It scared me but I was also curious. The sensation was unlike anything I had ever felt—something between the thrill of a dream and the eerie detachment of a near-death experience. And at times, I would "see" or "hear" things out of the corner of my eye, or ear. Or just feel them in a more bodily, haptic way.

What followed was a voracious quest for understanding. I tried to replicate these experiences in every way I could think of. I looked for classes in philosophy, religion, history and literature that might address these events and tore through books by mystics, academics, and skeptics alike, seeking explanations. That's when I discovered Theosophy and the works of Charles Webster Leadbeater. His presentation of the wild world of astral planes and shimmering thought-forms was an open invitation for me and all of my friends to explore a whole new world.

My own adventure soon became more ambitions; it wasn't just about explaining moments of supposed disembodiment—it was the beginning of a journey into an entirely new understanding of reality itself, one that blended mind, spirit, and the physical world in ways I hadn't ever even heard of, much less thought possible.

What is Theosophy?

To appreciate the value of Leadbeater's contributions, we need to first back up a bit to understand Theosophy—a spiritual movement that emerged in the late 19th century. Practitioners offered an intricate cosmology that was designed to bridge the gap between Eastern mysticism and Western philosophy. Theosophy was not a religion; it was more of a worldview that combined the teachings of Hinduism, Buddhism, esoteric Christianity, and Western occultism into a unified system of thought. Theosophy sought to present a map of the universe that included interconnected planes of existence, layers of spiritual evolution, and the pursuit of universal truths that transcended individual religious doctrines and what we at times call "common sense."

To put this in context, we have to remember that Theosophy, as a self-described spiritual movement, emerged during a time marked by global imperialism and the rise of industrial capitalism. And these new technologies—and the management styles that accompanied them—were significantly reshaping the physical, political, and metaphysical landscapes of the world. So, in this sense, Theosophy was not just a religious or philosophical movement—it was also a response to the socio-political dynamics of an era defined by the complexities of empire, race, capitalism, and the uneasy meeting of East and West.

The late 19th century was a period of intense European colonial expansion, particularly by Britain, France, and other imperial powers. Much of the world, especially Asia, Africa, and the Middle East, was under colonial rule, and the scientific, cultural, and even religious hierarchies (Christianity, in particular) that underpinned these political adventures were deeply ingrained in Western thought. The Theosophical Society, founded in 1875 by the Russian mystic Helena Blavatsky and the American Spiritualist Henry Steel Olcott, arose within the backdrop of European exertion over vast swaths of the globe, acts often justified by a sense of, if not overtly stated, superiority grounded in both material and spiritual terminology.

Theosophy offered a challenge to the dominant Western narrative of imperialism, introducing an alternative cosmology that suggested the existence of higher spiritual planes and the inherent unity of all life. It was not, however, explicitly political nor was it a wholesale rejection of Western ideas. Theosophy was more of an attempt to create a third way that synthesized Eastern and Western philosophies.

By incorporating elements of Eastern mysticism—primarily from Hinduism and Buddhism—these intellectuals—practitioners, really—created a framework that subverted old skool Western materialism, offering wisdom that was well outside of the bounds of conventional Christian and Enlightenment thinking.

However, the Theosophists' approach to the East was not entirely without its contradictions. These thinkers often viewed Eastern religions and philosophies through a lens of romanticism and mysticism, a phenomenon that would later be roundly critiqued by scholars like Edward Said. But at the time, Theosophy represented a fascination with and appropriation of Eastern thought, albeit in a manner that tacitly presented the West as an "enlightened" force bringing Eastern wisdom to a materialistic world.

Theosophists were intrigued by ancient Eastern teachings, but they often adapted and reframed these teachings through a Western lens. For instance, while Blavatsky's work made extensive use of Hindu and Buddhist ideas, she interpreted them through a framework of universalism that fit within a Western intellectual tradition of syncretism. And while this opened new ways of thinking about spirituality, it engaged in a form of remediation or, more pejoratively, "spiritual colonization," by reshaping Eastern teachings to fit the expectations of a European audience. On the other hand, how else were they to communicate these radically different ideas to their Western audience, many of whom were far less worldly than they?

In addition to the cultural climate, new technologies in the late 19th century were re-shaping the intellectual landscape in which

Theosophy emerged. Photography, in particular, played a key role in the Western exploration of both the physical and metaphysical world.

The development of photographic techniques offered new ways of documenting reality; and it spurred interest in capturing the hitherto fore invisible. Photographers and scientists, including anthropologists, began experimenting with "spirit photography," attempting to photograph ghosts and spiritual entities, while other inventors and thinkers worked on technologies like x-rays and early forms of motion pictures to peer into unseen realms. Subsequently, these technologies totally transformed how we understand the world.

A recent exhibit, The Perfect Medium: Photography and the Occult, at the Metropolitan Museum of Art in New York presented some of this early work. When I walked into The Perfect Medium, I was captivated. The exhibit showcased photographs that blurred the line between the physical world and the unseen— images of spirits and mediums caught on film, a fusion of photography and the supernatural.

One image by William Mumler showed Mary Lincoln with her husband standing behind her, a hand on her shoulder. Another featured French illusionist Henry Robin in 1863 posing with a ghost. I was drawn to this work by Robin (see below), and I purchased a print of his work from the show. It felt like a manifestation of Robin's personal connection to another world. Ever since, I've been interested in spirit photography—and the idea that technology could introduce us to realms beyond what we can see.

It might seem quaint today to try to use film to capture ghosts, but we are still working with technologies—some very advanced—to peer into the unseen, expand our capabilities, and learn to transcend the limits of our bodies and minds. Just as spirit photography in the 19th century attempted to capture the intangible, today's silicon technologies work towards this. Whether through virtual reality, microscopy, neuroscience, or AI, we search for ways to access realms beyond the everyday. It is glaringly obvious that the knowledge we have today is just a tiny fraction of what can be understood.

Photograph by William Mumler showing a seated Mary Lincoln with the ghost of
her husband Abraham Lincoln behind her.

Relatedly, much of what is considered to be limitations are, in fact, just cultural constructs. What we think of as boundaries often reflect the current state of our knowledge and thinking, and not the true potential that lies ahead as we continue to explore. In this sense, these photos can, perhaps counter-intuitively, be read more as mirrors of their makers, rather than as windows into other times and spaces.

Photography thus became a tool for reaching into the realm of spirits and the unseen, but also as a refraction of the way that Mumler and others understood it at the time. In a similar vein, parapsychological research in the 20th century, funded at celebrated institutions like Duke University and Stanford University, explored phenomena that interested scientists of the times, such as telepathy, clairvoyance, lucid dreaming, and remote viewing. In studies there, students worked to use scientific methods to measure and document extrasensory perception (ESP), shifting what was once considered the mystical into the realm of scientific inquiry.

At Duke, Joseph B. Rhine's experiments with Zener cards sought to quantify telepathy, while at Stanford, Hal Puthoff's work on remote viewing aimed to demonstrate that people could access information about distant locations without relying on their physical senses. These studies were in many ways the modern scientific extension of earlier spiritualist pursuits.

This research, particularly into phenomena like telepathy and psychokinesis, faced increasing criticism from both the scientific community as well as from state and public actors, and it was eventually shuttered. Institutional research into paranormal phenomena, such as remote viewing and telekinesis, may simply be inherently flawed because the fundamental worldview that defines traditional scientific methods often conflicts with the nature of these experiences.

It is worth noting that while the aim of these studies was scientific, they attracted the interest of government agencies like DARPA due to the potential military applications of parapsychological phenomena. The *Stargate Project (1977)*, for instance, investigated military applications for remote viewing, further cementing the idea that the human mind might be capable of transcending physical limits, much as the Theosophists and spiritualists had suggested a century earlier. But perhaps this, the desire to use these methods instrumentally, solely for political gain, is the real reason this fascinating work failed to achieve its goals within military contexts.

A less loaded explanation for the failure of these programs lies in the use of modernist scientific methods. Identifying and "measuring" extra-ordinary occurrences, which challenge Newtonian concepts of space, time, and material reality, require starting from a non-local, subjective approach to consciousness that conventional research methods cannot really accommodates. And of course, the tools used to track parapsychological events were rooted in a materialistic worldview, which struggles to validate, much less capture, phenomena that transcends the physical world as we usually experience it. As a result, methods focused on empirical observation and controlled environments are almost guaranteed to fall short in studying non-material, non-local experiences.

Even so, we continue to see science being wielded in similar ways. For example, in the field of neuroscience, researchers have been mapping the brain's responses to experiences such as near-death experiences (NDEs), out-of-body experiences (OBEs), and even astral projection. Technologies like fMRI scans allow researchers to study brain activity during these events, possibly providing a glimpse into the neural processes of the brain that may be at work when someone "leaves" their body.

But here, as you probably noted to yourself, mind and brain are paired in ways that may not end up being all that helpful.

At any rate, this research represents a scientific extension of trying to document phenomena once considered spiritual or paranormal. Just as spirit photography and parapsychology tried to harness the power of technology to probe the unseen world, today's tools—neuroscience, and even VR ad AI to an extent—push us to ask new questions about ourselves, the nature of consciousness, the afterlife, and even extraterrestrial life. We continue our quest to transcend physical reality whether it's through the lens of a camera or the scan of a brain. And these newer technologies, limited as they are by the ideologies of the enlightenment, carry forward the same enduring human curiosity that fueled the Theosophists' and spiritualists' work a century ago in the first place.

The Theosophical movement, with its emphasis on a non-linear understanding of consciousness stoked human powers. Theosophists explored other planes of existence and "thought-forms"—thoughts and emotions that have tangible, visible manifestations—paralleling the rise of photography. Far from the nostalgic luddites looking to limit one to the days of yore, they were fascinated by emerging film arts, and other inventions, like the telegraph and early radio, that were dramatically re-shaping the popular imagination. And of course, the Industrial Revolution was the techno-political lever operating in the world at this time. But Theosophists' emphasis on spiritual evolution and the pursuit of universal truth resonated with people disillusioned by the dehumanizing effects of industrialization.

As the Western world became increasingly dominated by capitalism, and industrialism—and alongside it, mass production, urbanization, ecological destruction, and the mechanization of labor—many intellectuals, artists, and philosophers questioned the direction Western society was taking. The rise of Theosophy was part and parcel of this larger reckoning, offering an alternative to bourgeois materialism and the crass instrumentalization of life required by industrial capitalism.

As capitalism became increasingly exploitative—especially in colonial contexts where labor and resources were extracted to fuel primitive accumulation and industrial production at home—Theosophy took on the role of a spiritual corrective to an economic system that perpetuated and depended on inequality and oppression. Ironically, these same socio-economic conditions allowed for the Western interest in the "otherness" of Eastern cultures to blossom. Theosophists were entranced by Eastern philosophies, but they also wanted to incorporate these ancient systems of thought into the rapidly changing social fabric of the West.

Theosophists were looking for a way to enter into the supposedly exotic cultures of the Ease while addressing the social and spiritual upheavals that accompanied the rise of Western-led capitalism. Of course, the movement was led by a coterie of different kinds of thinkers, but overall, Theosophy embodied the tensions of its time. It was responding to the contradictions of Western colonialism and industrialism by seeking a universal spiritual vision that transcended the limits of materialism.

And globalization was creating new opportunities for meetings of hearts and minds, especially though the introduction of Indian worldviews to the West. For example, Swami Vivekananda's electrifying speech at the 1893 Parliament of the World's Religions in Chicago marked a pivotal moment in the West's encounter with Hindu philosophy.

His message of unity resonated with Theosophical ideals; he became a portal to Eastern mysticism for Western intellectuals like C.W. Leadbeater. They shared with Vivekananda a vision of the spiritual world as an arena of profound order, purpose, and potential—not a place of superstition and mystification.

Today, with our world marked at every turn by ecological collapse, digital disconnection, and cultural fracturing, Vivekananda's call for unity resonates more deeply than ever before. His message is as spiritual as it is practical: humanity's future depends on recognizing the interconnection of all life and embracing the potential for collective spiritual evolution.

But what about Leadbeater and the Astral Plane? C.W. Leadbeater was more than just a Theosophist—he was a visionary. A clergyman turned mystic, his work combined scholarly curiosity with the imagination of an artist. But for him, the astral plane was not some woo-woo abstraction but a tangible realm, full of color, light, and energy—a real place where thought, emotion, and spirit manifested in physical forms. A place that requires careful travel, and the correct intentions.

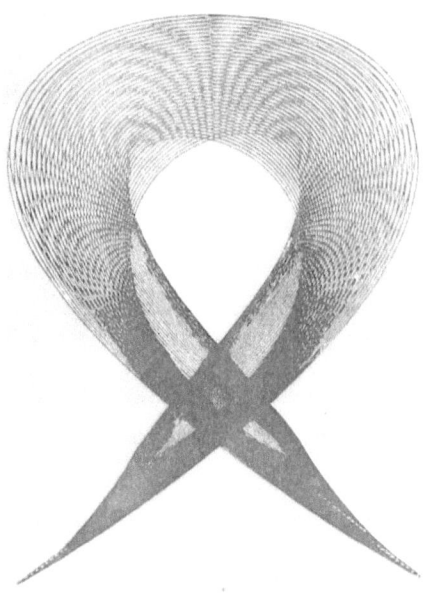

Form #38 / Aspiration to Enfold All

Leadbeater's characterization of the astral plane as a realm of heightened perception stared with recognizing the ways that human consciousness can transcend the limitations of the physical body. He proposed that through practice, anyone could access this realm and explore its vast dimensions.

His writings were not just theoretical; they were pragmatic, offering guidance into how one can navigate the astral world. Leadbeater often spoke of roaming to distant places, meeting other travelers, and encountering higher beings. He believed that these experiences were not only possible but essential for spiritual growth and self-realization. One of the most intriguing aspects of Leadbeater's work was his work with *thought-forms*—thoughts and emotions that have a tangible, energetic reality.

Annie Besant, one of Theosophy's most influential figures, was both an intellectual powerhouse and a tireless social activist. She partnered with Leadbeater to co-author a book on *Thought-Forms* (1905); it turned out to be a monumental contribution. Their exploration of the invisible forces shaping our world—emotions, thoughts, and spiritual energy—would go on to influence not just religious philosophy, but the way we conceptualize the unseen realms.

In *Thought-Forms*, Leadbeater and Besant described and provided incredible colorful illustrations of these phenomena, depicting thoughts and emotions as swirling, colorful shapes. A loving thought might appear as a soft, glowing pink cloud, while anger, for example, might manifest as jagged red lines.

Leadbeater's vivid descriptions of these shapes showed how consciousness itself has a physical component, one that interacts with the world in ways far beyond our usual understanding. And although Leadbeater's ideas have been dismissed by materialist skeptics, for those who have undertaken astral projection, his words feel eerily familiar. For me, this work provided a scaffold through which I could make sense of some of my own experiences.

Perhaps *thought*, after all, has a weight, texture, and motion—a ontological proposition not typically found in Western circles.

With talks and the publication of books, Theosophy's popularity in the West reflected a growing interest in esoteric abilities and non-ordinary states of consciousness. Among other key figures contributing to this trend was Swami Panchadasi, a teacher whose works on clairvoyance, the astral world, and occult powers attracted practitioners who wanted to nurture their psychic faculties.

Swami Panchadasi's *Clairvoyance and Occult Powers* (1916) presents a detailed approach to developing clairvoyance (the ability to see beyond the physical plane), telepathy, and astral projection. Unlike some of the more abstract, philosophical discussions of astral realms, Panchadasi provided step-by-step instructions for exploring the metaphysical world. He focused on cultivating the ability to sense and perceive the subtle energies of the astral plane and beyond, with an emphasis on real-world exercises that lead to direct experience. Panchadasi's teachings on astral projection emphasized that the astral body (or "double") was capable of separating from the physical body and traveling to distant locations, experiencing other dimensions, and entering past and future timelines.

Clairvoyance and Occult Powers stresses the importance of self-discipline, caution, and ethical clarity when accessing these powers. Like the Theosophical view that these special abilities should be used for advancing spiritual wisdom for the benefit of humanity, Panchadasi was deeply concerned with ensuring that students approached occult knowledge with a sense of responsibility. In many ways, Panchadasi's opus is a crossover between some of the more arcane writings of Theosophy and the growing New Age movement of the early 20th century which built upon these concepts. These ideas influenced the next of seekers who would remix Theosophical teachings with modern scientific theories and Eastern spiritual practices, much in the same way that more contemporary figures like Stanislav Grof and Carlos Castaneda do in their explorations of altered states of consciousness.

Carlos Castaneda's work, particularly his early writings on his apprenticeship with the Yaqui shaman Don Juan Matus, adds a fascinating layer to the exploration of altered states of consciousness, and especially astral travel. Castaneda's highly entertaining first books, *The Teachings of Don Juan* (1968) and A *Separate Reality* (1971), introduced readers to a worldview in which the boundaries of perception can be altered through the use of psychotropic substances like peyote and mushrooms, guiding the initiate into higher realms of awareness.

The controversies surrounding Castaneda's entrance—or non-entrance—into academia are legendary. While it is not worth diverting our focus here to examine his life story, it does merit attention. The methodologies he used for his fieldwork were considered unconventional and unscientific by many, and some scholars questioned whether his work qualified as legitimate anthropological research.

The broader academic community remained divided: some viewed his work as innovative and thought-provoking, while others dismissed it as fictional and misleading. Regardless, I cannot overstate the significance of insights presented in his work.

In Castaneda's work, these altered states resemble the realms encountered by those experiencing astral projection. Under the guidance of Don Juan, Castaneda learns to "see" beyond the ordinary perception of the world, entering what he calls non-ordinary reality. This world is marked by its own logic, populated by entities that exist beyond the regular physical world—a characteristic of many astral experiences, where one encounters otherworldly figures or enter mystical dimensions.

And although Castaneda's early works center on his pointedly sacred use of hallucinogenic substances to access these realms, he identifies the metaphysical focus that astral projection embodies. As Castaneda learns, the key is not merely to "escape" the body but rather to to break free of the limitations of perception and open oneself to a more fluid and expansive experience. His later works—particularly *The Art of Dreaming* (1993)—examine dream states, where the borderlines between dream and reality blur. Castaneda's dream work extends to other out-of-body experiences, where travelers report navigating non-ordinary environments.

What is central to Castaneda's teaching is the idea of shifting perception. Castaneda describes how, by using techniques like inhabiting a dreaming body and focusing on "seeing" in a different way, one can enter alternative states that transcend workaday physical restrictions. Reports on journeys beyond the envelope off the skin show us a glimpse into the higher consciousness that awaits all of us.

The question of what consciousness is, how it works, and whether or to what extent or in what way it exists independently of the physical body has intrigued both scientists and mystics for centuries. Theosophists focused on the states of consciousness that connect individuals to universal truths. In recent years, neuroscientific approaches to consciousness—such as the exploration of altered states through psychedelics—have led to new insights into the nature of subjective experience. The resurgence on psychedelic research, notably by figures like Roland Griffiths, Stanislav Grof, and Michael Pollen is fascinating on this point.

The potential to use substances like psilocybin and DMT in a therapeutic setting is opening new pathways for investigating "mystical experiences" that were once central to Theosophical inquiry. Today, these substances are being studied under controlled scientific conditions to explore their effects on consciousness, heath and healing, and spirituality. I would add, this is often for the benefit of pharmaceutical companies or economic gain. I wonder if this research will encounter similar conceptual and methodological challenges that once hindered parapsychology, particularly when attempting to reconcile subjective, non-linear experiences with the empirical rigor and language requested of scientific frameworks. Sometimes, these mismatches result in failure to quantify or neologisms that science funders may not like.

Stanislav Grof, a Czech psychiatrist and founder of transpersonal psychology, is best known for his pioneering research into non-ordinary states of consciousness, particularly through the use of what he called "holotropic" breathwork and psychedelic therapy. In many ways, the work of Grof has extended and deepened the exploration of altered states of consciousness, building on the foundations laid by figures like Leadbeater and the Theosophists.

Grof's studies, particularly those involving the effects of LSD and other psychedelics, explained states of awareness that had been central to mystical traditions for millennia. But his special approach to consciousness goes beyond the individual mind to consider the transpersonal dimensions of experience. Grof advances the idea that consciousness is not confined to the body but is part of a larger, interconnected cosmic fabric. This perspective dovetails with Theosophy's emphasis on universal interconnectedness and the idea that spiritual growth transcends the limitations of the material world.

And just as Leadbeater offered practical descriptions of the astral plane, Grof maps the inner realms of consciousness, demonstrating how exploring these realms can lead to healing, transformation, and spiritual insight. The relationship between Grof's holotropic work and astral projection lies in their shared celebration of altered states of consciousness, though each approaches this exploration from slightly different perspective—Grof from a psychological and therapeutic standpoint, and astral projection from a mystical or metaphysical one. And Castaneda's teachings emphasize the shamanic use of altered perception to access higher realities for various ends. These three perspectives—scientific, therapeutic, mystical and experiential—highlight the many potentials of non-ordinary states of consciousness, making them an essential part of the ongoing conversation about astral projection and spiritual exploration.

So, why, in 2025, should anyone care about a relatively obscure 19th-century movement like Theosophy? The answer lies in its commitment to the interconnectedness of all things. In a world increasingly defined by division, disconnection, and fragmentation—be it through political polarization, neoliberal inequality, social media echo chambers, or the environmental crises that threaten our collective future—Theosophy offers a radical alternative: a vision of unity. This is not the unity of techno-economic globalization that seeks to flatten difference, but rather a celebration of beauty within the multiplicity.

Theosophy's principles are more than pollyannish philosophical musings—they are urgent calls to action. Now, as humanity stands on the brink of ecological collapse and faces unprecedented levels of fragmentation, Theosophy's emphasis on spiritual evolution, compassion, and connectedness offers a blueprint for collective healing. By recognizing the divine essence that unites all beings, we are encouraged to transcend superficial differences and work toward a future with a shared purpose.

Yes, this all sounds like a lot of pretty words. The real question is a pragmatic one. How are we actually going to do this? As people still very much committed to Enlightenment style epistemology, maybe science (despite the methodological mismatch we talked about above) remains our most promising apparatus. This is especially true when we consider how post-modern critiques of both science and language has led serious scholars to become far more reflexive, reconsidering the foundational terms of their work. Nowhere is this more important, and productive, than in the fields—physics, philosophy, biology, anthropology, and so on—that consider the phenomena of consciousness.

The philosopher David Chalmers is known for questioning and articulating the *"hard problem"* of consciousness, which explores why and how subjective experiences arise from physical processes (how mind arises from brain, and if that is indeed how it works!) To address this problem, Chalmers introduced the idea of the *philosophical zombie*—a hypothetical being that behaves identically to a human but lacks conscious experience. The *zombie* challenges materialist perspectives, as it underscores the difficulty of explaining subjective experience purely through physical mechanisms. Both Chalmers and Theosophical thinkers highlight the limitations of reductionist science in accounting for the full range of human experience, inviting us to imagine and engage upon a deeper exploration into the mysteries of mind, self, and reality.

Relatedly, contemporary neuroscientists have begun to seriously consider ideas that echo Theosophical principals. Sounding like Grof, Rupert Sheldrake's theory of morphic fields posits that consciousness is not merely an individual phenomenon, but a collective one that influences the patterns of life itself. This idea bears a striking resemblance to Leadbeater's notion of thought-forms. Quantum physics, too, with its many paradoxes and strange phenomena, suggests that the universe operates in ways that go way outside of conventional understandings.

This "new" universe is populated by many different types of energies and entities, as Leadbeater's *The Astral Plane* will outline. Likewise, Diana Walsh Pasulka's work, particularly in *American Cosmic: UFOs, Religion, Technology* explores how spirituality, science, technology, and consciousness meet from the perspective of the humanities. Elsewhere Pasulka describes how reports of encounters with UFOs and extraterrestrials seem to parallel religious and mystical traditions, framing them as part of an ongoing engagement with the unknown. She considers how contemporary phenomena open avenues for understanding consciousness in ways that integrate mysticism with science. What interests me most is her suggestion that these experiences are not necessarily anomalies, but windows into dimensions of reality that are often disregarded by Western society.

Just as Leadbeater described the astral plane as a realm of infinite possibilities, modern physics suggests that the universe far weirder and more wonderful than we ever could have imagined. What a relief!

Pasulka remains somewhat agnostic about the truth value of the evidence she presents, but she seems unsure what to make of the many claims people share regarding alien encounters, state collusion, and consciousness technologies. There are long passages of interview transcripts that I wish included more of her own commentary. Maybe this open-endedness is the book's real strength. She is a religious studies scholar, but I prefer to read Pasulka's work on alien encounters as an ethnography that fits within an anthropological trajectory. And, well, anthropological studies, especially those on non-Western societies, provide numerous accounts of nonlocal consciousness and nonordinary encounters.

In *The Cosmic Serpent*, for example, Jeremy Narby describes how Amazonian shamans use ritual ayahuasca to communicate with spirits and gain knowledge. Similarly, Michael Harner's *The Way of the Shaman* describes out-of-body experiences during trance states in which healers embark on spiritual journeys to access insights for healing. The shaman depicted on the previous page has prepared for an astral adventure by restricting his diet, sleep, and habits of thought and movement.

Wade Davis, in works like *The Serpent and the Rainbow* and *One River*, highlights the role of plant-based hallucinogens, technologies if you will, in enabling visions and dream-states that conflate subjective experience and shared reality. Ayahuasca ceremonies, often guided by shamans, involve contact with otherworldly entities, ancestral spirits, or temporal-landscapes beyond ordinary perception.

Tibetan Buddhist practices, as those detailed in Robert Thurman's *The Tibetan Book of the Dead*, describe meditators achieving similar states of "clear light." Meanwhile, David Presti and B. Alan Wallace's *Mind Beyond Brain* examine telepathic experiences in Tibetan traditions, emphasizing their role in spiritual development.

These examples reveal a sizable array of practices, largely unknown to most Westerners, that present challenges to Western ideological paradigms, foregrounding consciousness as a phenomenon that extends well beyond the physical body and that operates on principles that simply cannot be accounted for using Newtonian laws. Luckily for us, anthropology, with its focus on deconstructing the foundations of Western intellectual history, is uniquely suited to welcoming experiences often dismissed by dominant epistemologies.

Practices such as *astral projection*—an English term for what many cultures understand as a normal and legitimate aspect of spiritual and experiential life—are thus central to anthropological inquiry.

For example, Michelle Stephen's work on the Mekeo of Papua New Guinea, particularly in her fabulous ethnography *Asia's Gifts*, documents the practice of "soul journeys," which involve traversing different realms of existence. Stephen explains how the Mekeo engage in intentional practices that enable their "souls" to leave their bodies during sleep or trance states. Shamans interact with ancestors, seek guidance, skip time, and influence the physical world, which, in their view, is largely shaped by events occurring in the astral plane.

Astral experiences are central to the fundamental ontological framework—how the Mekeo understand the nature of reality—and they undoubtedly trouble Western "common sense." And these case studies are not outliers. Mircea Eliade's *Shamanism: Archaic Techniques of Ecstasy* and Holger Kalweit's *Dreamtime and Inner Space* also explore psychic phenomena across diverse cultural traditions.

And along with the increasingly weird Western commodification of spiritual activities such as yoga and meditation, Ford and McConville highlight how practices like astral projection and lucid dreaming are increasingly framed within Western capitalism as tools for self-improvement, productivity, and personal success (Ford 2019, McConville 2020). This neoliberalized approach to life reduces spiritual practices to self-help mechanisms, commodifying experiences that would otherwise contain the seeds for real cultural transformation.

Spiritual practices such as yoga, meditation, sound bathing, karate, horseback riding, long distance running, tantric sex, the use of psychotropics, dance, and so on have become merchandised and can be accessed like any other good. They are at risk becoming part of a broader consumer culture where branded experiences of transcendence are instrumentalized and geared toward personal gain.

This, as Ford and McConville argue, ultimately harms the individual by severing spiritual undertakings from their origins and turning them into identity badges or as products for self-optimization, which is often financialized. This is unfortunate because, as Wade Davis suggests, non-Western practices of nonlocal consciousness could show us a path for understanding the world and ourselves in ways that transcend tiresome Western consumerism (Davis 2018).

As the critical discipline par excellence, anthropology's willingness to take these practices seriously reveals cracks in modernist epistemologies and embraces the possibility that our methods for both knowing and shaping the world are, at best, partial.

Leadbeater, with his distinctly anthropological stance, sought to re-learn the ways of the world through personal engagement with esoteric traditions, aiming to map unseen realms and challenge the limits of Western knowledge systems.

Theosophy is not just a dusty relic from the past. It is a *living* philosophy—it offers a framework for approaching the mysteries of the universe and for tapping into human consciousness. I myself just stumbled into astral projection and lucid dreaming without really knowing what was going on.

When I first came across C.W. Leadbeater's *The Astral Plane*, it was a total game-changer. For the first time, I had a way to make a lot more sense out of what I was seeing, hearing, and feeling. His descriptions of the astral plane gave me a framework to understand my experiences, which had always felt so abstract and overwhelming.

What stood out the most were some of the practical advice he shared. This wasn't just about theory—it was about learning how to approach non-local consciousness with intention and focus. His insights helped me go beyond drifting into the astral; they suggested ways to navigate it with clarity and purpose. It became an issue of refining my awareness and truly working to open myself to the space I was stepping into.

One of the biggest lessons I took away from his work was that this kind of activity requires preparation. The astral plane is sacred and powerful, and it asks for respect and intentionality. Reading Leadbeater's work taught me how to approach these experiences not just as explorations, but as meaningful, spiritual undertakings.

So, if you're trying to navigate realities beyond boring old ordinary perception, this book is for you!

- Lula Crowder

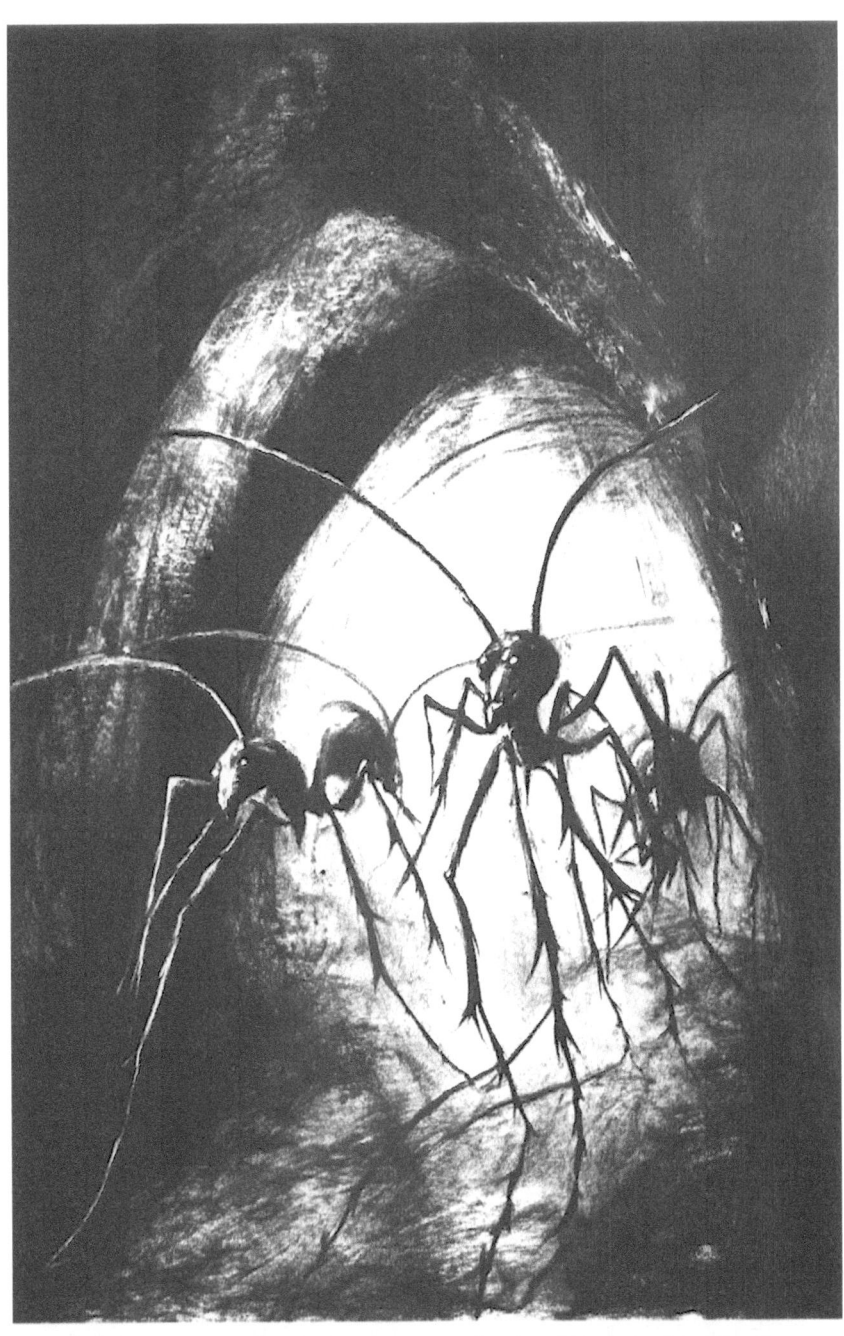

Most people do not realize that ants are our closest spiritual cousins. They have a great deal to teach us about dreaming, projection, and design. Ants are as wise as they are powerful. Seek their guidance.

1

PREFACE.

Few words are needed in sending this little book out into the world. It is the fifth of a series of Manuals designed to meet the public demand for a simple exposition of Theosophical teachings. Some have complained that our literature is at once too abstruse, too technical, and too expensive for the ordinary reader, and it is our hope that the present series may succeed in supplying what is a very real want. Theosophy is not only for the learned; it is for all. Perhaps among those who in these little books catch their first glimpse of its teachings, there may be a few who will be led by them to penetrate more deeply into its philosophy, its science and its religion, facing its more abstruse problems with the student's zeal and the neophyte's ardor. But these Manuals are not written for the eager student, whom no initial difficulties can daunt; they are written for the busy men and women of the work-a-day world and seek to make plain some of the great truths that render life easier to bear and death easier to face. Written by servants of the Masters who are the Elder Brothers of our race, they can have no other object than to serve our fellow men.

CWL

With intention, we can embrace our instincts, our subtle minds, and the spiritual
guides that surround us.

THE ASTRAL PLANE.

Paradox, koan, aphorism—each reveals the limitations in language and reason.
Nietzsche and Bashō used these forms to open pathways to different knowings.
Here, minds are as individual as they are multiple.

2

INTRODUCTION.

Reference to the astral plane, or Kâmaloka as it is called in Sanskrit, has frequently been made by Theosophical writers, and a good deal of information on the subject of this realm of nature is to be found scattered here and there in our books; but there is not, so far as I am aware, any single volume to which one can turn for a complete summary of the facts at present known to us about this interesting region.

The object of this manual is to collect and make some attempt to arrange this scattered information, and to supplement it slightly in cases where new facts have come to our knowledge. It must be understood that any such additions are only the result of the investigations of a few explorers, and must not, therefore, be taken as in any way authoritative, but are given simply for what they are worth.

On the other hand, every precaution in our power has been taken to ensure accuracy, no fact, old or new, being admitted to this manual unless it has been confirmed by the testimony of at least two independent trained investigators among ourselves and has also been passed as correct by older students whose knowledge on these points is necessarily much greater than ours. It is hoped, therefore, that this account of the astral plane, though it cannot be considered as quite complete, may yet be found reliable as far as it goes.

The first point which it is necessary to make clear in describing this astral plane is its absolute *reality*. Of course in using that word I am not speaking from that metaphysical standpoint from which all but the One Unmanifested is unreal because impermanent; I am using the word in its plain, every-day sense, and I mean by it that the objects and inhabitants of the astral plane are real in exactly the same way as our own bodies, our furniture, our houses or monuments are real—as real as Charing Cross, to quote an expressive remark from one of the earliest Theosophical works.

They will no more endure forever than will objects on the physical plane, but they are nevertheless realities from our point of view while they last—realities which we cannot afford to ignore merely because the majority of mankind is as yet unconscious, or but vaguely conscious, of their existence.

There appears to be considerable misunderstanding even among Theosophical students upon this question of the reality of the various planes of the universe. This may perhaps be partly due to the fact that the word "plane" has occasionally been very loosely used in our literature—writers speaking vaguely of the mental plane, the moral plane, and so on; and this vagueness has led many people to suppose that the information on the subject which is to be found in Theosophical books is inexact and speculative—a mere hypothesis incapable of definite proof. No one can get a clear conception of the teachings of the Wisdom-Religion until he has at any rate an intellectual grasp of the fact that in our solar system there exist perfectly definite planes, each with its own matter of different degrees of density, and that some of these planes can be visited and observed by persons who have qualified themselves for the work, exactly as a foreign country might be visited and observed; and that, by comparison of the observations of those who are constantly working on these planes, evidence can be obtained of their existence and nature at least as satisfactory as that which most of us have for the existence of Greenland or Spitzbergen.

The names usually given to these planes, taking them in order of materiality, rising from the denser to the finer, are the physical, the astral, the devachanic, the sushuptic, and the nirvânic. Higher than this last are two others, but they are so far above our present power of conception that for the moment they may be left out of consideration.

Now it should be understood that the matter of each of these planes differs from that of the one below it in the same way as, though to a much greater degree than, vapor differs from solid matter; in fact, the states of matter which we call solid, liquid, and gaseous are merely the three lowest subdivisions of the matter belonging to this one physical plane.

The astral region which I am to attempt to describe is the second of these great planes of nature—the next above (or within) that physical world with which we are all familiar. It has often been called the realm of illusion—not that it is itself any more illusory than the physical world, but because of the extreme unreliability of the impressions brought back from it by the untrained seer.

This is to be accounted for mainly by two remarkable characteristics of the astral world—first, that many of its inhabitants have a marvelous power of changing their forms with Protean rapidity, and also of casting practically unlimited glamour over those with whom they choose to sport; and secondly, that sight on that plane is a faculty very different from and much more extended than physical vision. An object is seen, as it were, from all sides at once, the inside of a solid being as plainly open to the view as the outside; it is therefore obvious that an inexperienced visitor to this new world may well find considerable difficulty in understanding what he really does see, and still more in translating his vision into the very inadequate language of ordinary speech.

A good example of the sort of mistake that is likely to occur is the frequent reversal of any number which the seer must read from the astral light, so that he would be liable to render, say, 139 as 931, and so on. In the case of a student of occultism trained by a capable Master such a mistake would be impossible except through great hurry or carelessness, since such a pupil has to go through a long and varied course of instruction in this art of seeing correctly, the Master, or perhaps some more advanced pupil, bringing before him again and again all possible forms of illusion, and asking him "What do you see?" Any errors in his answers are then corrected and their reasons explained, until by degrees the neophyte acquires a certainty and confidence in dealing with the phenomena of the astral plane which far exceeds anything possible in physical life.

But he has to learn not only to see correctly but to translate the memory of what he has seen accurately from one plane to the other. And to assist him in this he is trained to carry his consciousness without break from the physical plane to the astral or devachanic and back again, for until that can be done there is always a possibility that his recollections may be partially lost or distorted during the blank interval which separates his periods of consciousness on the various planes. When the power of bringing over the consciousness is perfectly acquired the pupil will have the advantage of the use of all the astral faculties, not only while out of his body during sleep or trance, but also while fully awake in ordinary physical life.

It has been the custom of some Theosophists to speak with scorn of the astral plane and treat it as entirely unworthy of attention; but that seems to me a somewhat mistaken view. Most assuredly that at which we must aim is the purely spiritual plane, and it would be most disastrous for any student to neglect that higher development and rest satisfied with the attainment of astral consciousness.

There are some whose Karma is such as to enable them to develop the purely spiritual faculties first of all—to over-leap the astral plane for the time, as it were; and when afterwards they make its acquaintance they have, if their spiritual development has been perfect, the immense advantage of dipping into it from above, with the aid of a spiritual insight which cannot be deceived and a spiritual strength which nothing can resist.

It is, however, a mistake to suppose, as some writers have done, that this is the only, or even the ordinary method adopted by the Masters of Wisdom with their pupils. Where it is possible it saves much trouble, but for most of us such progress by leaps and bounds has been forbidden by our own faults or follies in the past: all that we can hope for is to win our way slowly step by step, and since this astral plane lies next to our world of denser matter, it is usually in connection with it that our earliest superphysical experiences take place.

It is therefore by no means without interest to those of us who are but beginners in these studies, and a clear comprehension of its mysteries may often be of the greatest importance to us, not only by enabling us to understand many of the phenomena of the *séance*-room, of haunted houses, etc., which would otherwise be inexplicable, but also to guard ourselves and others from possible dangers.

The first introduction to this remarkable region comes to people in various ways. Some only once in their whole lives under some unusual influence become sensitive enough to recognize the presence of one of its inhabitants, and perhaps, because the experience does not repeat itself, come in time to believe that on that occasion they must have been the victims of hallucination. Others find themselves with increasing frequency seeing and hearing something to which those around them are blind and deaf. Others again—and perhaps this is the commonest experience of all—begin to recollect with greater and greater clearness that which they have seen or heard on that other plane during sleep.

Among those who make a study of these subjects, some try to develop the astral sight by crystal-gazing or other methods, while those who have the inestimable advantage of the direct guidance of a qualified teacher will probably be placed upon that plane for the first time under his special protection, which will be continued until, by the application of various tests, he has satisfied himself that the pupil is proof against any danger or terror that he is likely to encounter. But however it may occur, the first actual realization that we are all the while in the midst of a great world full of active life, of which most of us are nevertheless entirely unconscious, cannot but be to some extent a memorable epoch in a man's existence.

So abundant and so manifold is this life of the astral plane that at first it is absolutely bewildering to the neophyte; and even for the more practiced investigator it is no easy task to attempt to classify and to catalogue it.

If the explorer of some unknown tropical forest were asked not only to give a full account of the country through which he had passed, with accurate details of its vegetable and mineral productions, but also to state the genus and species of every one of the myriad insects, birds, beasts, and reptiles which he had seen, he might well shrink appalled at the magnitude of the undertaking. Yet even this affords no parallel to the embarrassments of the psychic investigator, for in his case matters are further complicated, first by the difficulty of correctly translating from that plane to this the recollection of what he has seen, and secondly by the utter inadequacy of ordinary language to express much of what he has to report.

However, just as the explorer on the physical plane would probably commence his account of a country by some sort of general description of its scenery and characteristics, so it will be well to begin this slight sketch of the astral plane by endeavoring to give some idea of the scenery which forms the background of its marvelous and ever-changing activities. Yet here at the outset an almost insuperable difficulty confronts us in the extreme complexity of the matter.

All who see fully on that plane agree that to attempt to call up before those whose eyes are as yet unopened a vivid picture of this astral scenery is like speaking to a blind man of the exquisite variety of tints in a sunset sky—however detailed and elaborate the description may be, there is no certainty that the idea presented before the hearer's mind will be an adequate representation of the truth.

From his sculptures to the Sistine Chapel's cosmic narrative, Michelangelo's art maps the body anatomically and as a vessel for divine energy; his work is in uncanny alignment with the principles of chakras and astral planes, mapped here.
Sacred geometries abound.

3

SCENERY.

First of all, then, it must be understood that the astral plane has seven subdivisions, each of which has its corresponding degree of materiality and its corresponding condition of matter. Now numbering these from the highest and least material downwards, we find that they naturally fall into three classes, divisions 1, 2 and 3 forming one such class, and 4, 5 and 6 another, while the seventh and lowest of all stands alone. The difference between the matter of one of these classes and the next would be commensurable with that between a solid and a liquid, while the difference between the matter of the subdivisions of a class would rather resemble that between two kinds of solid, such as, say, steel and sand.

Putting aside for the moment the seventh, we may say that divisions 4, 5 and 6 of the astral plane have for their background the physical world we live in and all its familiar accessories. Life on the sixth division is simply our ordinary life on this earth, minus the physical body and its necessities; while as it ascends through the fifth and fourth divisions it becomes less and less material and is more and more withdrawn from our lower world and its interests.

The scenery of these lower divisions, then, is that of the earth as we know it: but it is also very much more; for when looked at from this different standpoint, with the assistance of the astral senses, even purely physical objects present a very different appearance. As has already been mentioned, they are seen by one whose eyes are fully opened, not as usual from one point of view, but from all sides at once—an idea in itself sufficiently confusing; and when we add to this that every particle in the interior of a solid body is as fully and clearly visible as those on the outside, it will be comprehended that under such conditions even the most familiar objects may at first be totally unrecognizable.

Yet a moment's consideration will show that such vision approximates much more closely to true perception than does physical sight. Looked at on the astral plane, for example, the sides of a glass cube would all appear equal, as they really are, while on the physical plane we see the further side in perspective—that is, it appears smaller than the nearer side, which is, of course, a mere illusion. It is this characteristic of astral vision which has led to its sometimes being spoken of as sight in the fourth dimension—a very suggestive and expressive phrase.

But in addition to these possible sources of error, matters are further complicated by the fact that astral sight cognizes forms of matter which, while still purely physical, are nevertheless invisible under ordinary conditions. Such, for example, are the particles composing the atmosphere, all the various emanations which are always being given out by everything that has life, and also four grades of a still finer order of physical matter which, for want of more distinctive names, must all he described as etheric. The latter form a kind of system by themselves, freely interpenetrating all other physical matter; and the investigation of their vibrations and the manner in which various higher forces affect them would in itself constitute a vast field of deeply interesting study for any man of science who possessed the requisite sight for its examination.

Even when our imagination has fully grasped all that is comprehended in what has already been said, we do not yet understand half the complexity of the problem. For besides all these new forms of

physical matter we have to deal with the still more numerous and per-
plexing subdivisions of astral matter. We must note first that every
material object, every particle even, has its astral counterpart; and this
counterpart is itself not a simple body, but is usually extremely complex, being composed of various kinds of astral matter. In addition to
this, each living creature is surrounded with an atmosphere of its own,
usually called its aura, and in the case of human beings this aura forms
of itself a very fascinating branch of study. It is seen as an oval mass
of luminous mist of highly complex structure, and from its shape has
sometimes been called the auric egg.

Theosophical readers will hear with pleasure that even at the early
stage of his development at which the pupil begins to acquire this
astral sight, he is able to assure himself by direct observation of the
accuracy of the teaching given through our great founder, Madame
Blavatsky, on the subject of some at least of the seven principles of
man. In regarding his fellow-man he no longer sees only his outer appearance; exactly co-extensive with that physical body he clearly distinguishes the etheric double, which in Theosophical literature has
usually been called the Linga Sharîra; while the Jîva, as it is absorbed
and specialized into Prâna, as it circulates in rosy light throughout the
body, as it eventually radiates from the healthy person in its altered
form, is also perfectly obvious.

Most brilliant and most easily seen of all, perhaps, though belonging to quite a different order of matter—the astral—is the kâmic aura,
which expresses by its vivid and ever-changing flashes of color the different desires which sweep across the man's mind from moment to
moment. This is the true astral body. Behind that and consisting of a
finer grade of matter—that of the rûpa levels of Devachan—lies the
devachanic body or aura of the lower Manas, whose colors, changing
only by slow degrees as the man lives his life, show the disposition
and character of the personality. While still higher and infinitely more
beautiful, where at all clearly developed, is the living light of the
Kârana Sharîra, the aura or vehicle of the higher Manas, which shows

the stage of development of the real Ego in its passage from birth to birth. But to be able to see these, the pupil must have developed something more than mere astral vision.

It will save the student much trouble if he learns at once to regard these auras not as mere emanations, but as the actual manifestation of the Ego on their respective planes—if he understands that it is the auric egg which is the real man, not the physical body which on this plane crystallizes in the middle of it. So long as the reincarnating Ego remains upon the plane which is his true home in the arûpa levels of Devachan, the body which he inhabits is the Kârana Sharîra, but when he descends into the rûpa levels he must, in order to be able to function upon them, clothe himself in their matter; and the matter that he thus attracts to himself furnishes his devachanic or mind-body.

Similarly, descending into the astral plane he forms his astral or kâmic body out of its matter, though of course still retaining all the other bodies, and on his still further descent to this lowest plane of all the physical body is formed in the midst of the auric egg, which thus contains the entire man. Fuller accounts of these auras will be found in *Transaction* No. 18 of the London Lodge, and in a recent article of mine in *The Theosophist*, but enough has been said here to show that as they all occupy the same space (which by the way they share also with the physical health-aura), the finer interpenetrating the grosser, it needs careful study and much practice to enable the neophyte to distinguish clearly at a glance the one from the other. Nevertheless, the human aura, or more usually some one part of it only, is not infrequently one of the first purely astral objects seen by the untrained, though in such a case its indications are naturally very likely to be misunderstood.

Though the kâmic aura from the brilliancy of its flashes of color may often be more conspicuous, the nerve-ether and the etheric double are really of a much denser order of matter, being strictly speaking within the limits of the physical plane, though invisible to ordinary sight. It has been the custom in Theosophical literature to describe the

Linga Sharîra as the astral counterpart of the human body, the word "astral" having been usually applied to everything beyond the cognition of our physical senses.

As closer investigation enables us to be more precise in the use of our terms, however, we find ourselves compelled to admit much of this invisible matter as purely physical, and therefore to define the Linga Sharîra no longer as the astral, but as the etheric double. This seems an appropriate name for it, since it consists of various grades of that matter which scientists call "ether," though this proves on examination to be not a separate substance, as has been generally supposed, but a condition of finer subdivision than the gaseous, to which any kind of physical matter may be reduced by the application of the appropriate forces.

The name "etheric double" will therefore for the future be used in Theosophic writings instead of "Linga Sharîra." This change will not only give us the advantage of an English name which is clearly indicative of the character of the body to which it is applied, but will also relieve us from the frequent misunderstandings which have arisen from the fact that an entirely different signification is attached in all the Oriental books to the name we have hitherto been using.

It must not however be supposed that in making this alteration in nomenclature we are in any way putting forward a new conception. We are simply altering, for the sake of greater accuracy, the labels previously attached to certain facts in nature. If we examine with psychic faculty the body of a newly-born child, we shall find it permeated not only by astral matter of every degree of density, but also by the several grades of etheric matter; and if we take the trouble to trace these inner bodies backwards to their origin, we find that it is of the latter that the etheric double—the mold upon which the physical body is built up—is formed by the agents of the Lords of Karma; while the astral matter has been gathered together by the descending Ego—not of course consciously, but automatically—as he passes through the astral plane.

Into the composition of the etheric double must enter something of all the different grades of etheric matter; but the proportions may vary greatly, and are determined by several factors, such as the nation, tribe or type of a man, as well as by his individual Karma. When it is remembered that these four subdivisions of matter are made up of numerous combinations, which, in their turn, form aggregations that enter into the composition of the "atom" of the so-called "element" of the chemist, it will be seen that this second principle of man is highly complex, and the number of its possible variations practically infinite, so that, however complicated and unusual a man's Karma may be, the Lipika are able to give a mold in accordance with which a body exactly suiting it can be formed.

One other point deserves mention in connection with the appearance of physical matter when looked at from the astral plane, and that is that the astral vision possesses the power of magnifying at will the minutest physical particle to any desired size, as though by a microscope, though its magnifying power is enormously greater than that of any microscope ever made or ever likely to be made.

The hypothetical molecule and atom postulated by science are therefore visible realities to the occult student, though the latter recognizes them as much more complex in their nature than the scientific man has yet discovered them to be. Here again is a vast field of study of absorbing interest to which a whole volume might readily be devoted. A scientific investigator who should acquire this astral sight in perfection would not only find his experiments with ordinary and known phenomena immensely facilitated but would also see stretching before him entirely new vistas of knowledge needing more than a lifetime for their thorough examination. For example, one curious and very beautiful novelty brought to his notice by the development of this vision would be the existence of other and entirely different colors beyond the limits of the ordinarily visible spectrum, the ultra-red and ultra-violet rays which science has discovered by other means being plainly perceptible to astral sight. We must not, however, allow ourselves to follow these fascinating bye-paths, but must resume our endeavor to give a general idea of the appearance of the astral plane.

It will by this time be obvious that though, as above stated, the ordinary objects of the physical world form the background to life on certain levels of the astral plane, yet so much more is seen of their real appearance and characteristics that the general effect differs widely from that with which we are familiar. For the sake of illustration, take a rock as an example of the simpler class of objects.

When regarded with trained sight, a rock is no mere inert mass of stone. First of all, the whole of the physical matter of the rock is seen instead of a very small part of it; secondly, the vibrations of its physical particles are perceptible; thirdly, it is seen to possess an astral counterpart composed of various grades of astral matter, whose particles are also in constant motion; fourthly, the Jíva or universal life is seen to be circulating through it and radiating from it; fifthly, an aura will be seen surrounding it, though this is, of course, much less extended and varied than in the case of the higher kingdoms; sixthly, its appropriate elemental essence is seen permeating it, ever active but ever fluctuating. In the case of the vegetable, animal and human kingdoms, the complications are naturally much more numerous.

It may be objected by some readers that no such complexities as these are described by most of the psychics who occasionally get glimpses of the astral world, nor are they reported at *séances* by the entities that manifest there; but this is readily accounted for. Few untrained persons on that plane, whether living or dead, see things as they really are until after very long experience. Even those who do see fully are often too dazed and confused to understand or remember. And among the very small minority who both see and remember, there are hardly any who can translate the recollection into language on our lower plane. Many untrained psychics never examine their visions scientifically at all: they simply obtain an impression which may be quite correct, but may also be half false, or even wholly misleading.

All the more probable does the latter hypothesis become when we take into consideration the frequent tricks played by sportive denizens of the other world, against which the untrained person is usually absolutely defenseless. It must also be remembered that the regular inhabitant of the astral plane, whether he be human or elemental, is under ordinary circumstances conscious only of the objects of that plane, physical matter being to him as entirely invisible as is astral matter to the majority of mankind.

Since, as before remarked, every physical object has its astral counterpart, which *would* be visible to him, it may be thought that the distinction is a trivial one, yet it is an essential part of the symmetrical conception of the subject. If, however, an astral entity constantly works through a medium, these finer astral senses may gradually be so coarsened as to become insensible to the higher grades of matter on their own plane, and to include in their purview the physical world as we see it instead; but only the trained visitor from this life, who is fully conscious on both planes, can depend upon seeing both clearly and simultaneously. Be it understood, then, that the complexity exists, and that only when it is fully perceived and scientifically unraveled is there perfect security against deception or mistake.

For the seventh or lowest subdivision of the astral plane also this physical world of ours may be said to be the background, though what is seen is only a distorted and partial view of it, since all that is light and good and beautiful seems invisible. It was thus described four thousand years ago in the Egyptian papyrus of the Scribe Ani: "What manner of place is this unto which I have come? It hath no water, it hath no air; it is deep, unfathomable; it is black as the blackest night, and men wander helplessly about therein; in it a man may not live in quietness of heart." For the unfortunate entity on that level, it is indeed true that "all the earth is full of darkness and cruel habitations," but it is darkness which radiates from within himself and causes his existence to be passed in a perpetual night of evil and horror—a very real hell, though, like all other hells, entirely of man's own creation.

Most students find the investigation of this section an extremely unpleasant task, for there appears to be a sense of density and gross materiality about it which is indescribably loathsome to the liberated astral body, causing it the sense of pushing its way through some black, viscous fluid, while the inhabitants and influences encountered there are also usually exceedingly undesirable.

The first, second, and third subdivisions seem much further removed from this physical world, and correspondingly less material. Entities inhabiting these levels lose sight of the earth and its belongings; they are usually deeply self-absorbed, and to a large extent create their own surroundings, though these are not purely subjective, as in Devachan, but on the contrary sufficiently objective to be perceptible to other entities and also to clairvoyant vision. This region is beyond doubt the "summerland" of which we hear so much at spiritualistic *séances*, and the entities who descend from and describe it are probably often speaking the truth as far as their knowledge extends.

It is on these planes that "spirits" call into temporary existence their houses, schools, and cities, for these objects are often real enough for the time, though to a clearer sight they may sometimes be pitiably unlike what their delighted creators suppose them to be. Nevertheless, many of the imaginations that take form there are of real though temporary beauty, and a visitor who knew of nothing higher might wander contentedly enough there among forests and mountains, lovely lakes and pleasant flower-gardens, or might even construct such surroundings to suit his own fancies.

It may be said in passing that communication is limited on the astral plane by the knowledge of the entity, just as it is here. While a person able to function freely on that plane can communicate with any of the human entities there present more readily and rapidly than on earth, by means of mental impressions, the inhabitants themselves do not usually seem able to exercise this power but appear to be restricted by limitations similar to those that prevail on earth, though perhaps less rigid. The result of this is that they are found associating, there as here in groups drawn together by common sympathies, beliefs, and language.

An account of the scenery of the astral plane would be incomplete without mention of what are commonly called the Records of the Astral Light, the photographic representation of all that has ever happened. These records are really and permanently impressed upon that higher medium called the Âkâsha and are only reflected in a more or less spasmodic manner in the astral light, so that one whose power of vision does not rise above this plane will be likely to obtain only occasional and disconnected pictures of the past instead of a coherent narrative. But nevertheless, images of all kinds of past events are constantly being reproduced on the astral plane and form an important part of the surroundings of the investigator there.

For Kant, beauty is found in harmony &
form, something pleasing and contained,
but the sublime points toward the
terrific, the infinite, and the
incomprehensible. The astral plane
defies conventional understanding and
elicits awe. It is not a place to be
passively admired but one that confronts
us with our own limitations.

4

INHABITANTS.

Having sketched in, however slightly, the background of our picture, we must now attempt to fill in the figures—to describe the inhabitants of the astral plane. The immense variety of these entities makes it exceedingly difficult to arrange and tabulate them. Perhaps the most convenient method will be to divide them into three great classes, the human, the non-human, and the artificial.

HUMAN.

The human denizens of Kâmaloka fall naturally into two groups, the living and the dead, or, to speak more accurately, those who have still a physical body, and those who have not.

Living.

The entities which manifest on the astral plane during physical life may be subdivided into four classes: the Adept or Chela in the Mâyâvirûpa, the Psychically-developed Person, the Ordinary Person and lastly, the Black Magician or his pupil.

First, we consider *the Adept or Chela in the Mâyâvirûpa.*

This body is the artificial vehicle used on the four lower or rûpa divisions of the devachanic plane by those capable of functioning there during earth-life, and is formed out of the substance of the mind-body. The pupil is at first unable to construct this for himself, and has therefore to be content with his ordinary astral body composed of the less refined matter of the kâmic aura. But at a certain stage of his progress, the Master Himself forms his Mâyâvirûpa for him for the first time, and afterwards instructs and assists him until he can make it for himself easily and expeditiously.

When this facility is attained, this vehicle is habitually used in place of the grosser astral body, since it permits of instant passage from the astral to the devachanic plane and back again at will, and allows of the use at all times of the higher powers belonging to its own plane. It must be noted, however, that a person travelling in the Mâyâvirûpa is not perceptible to merely astral vision unless he chooses to make himself so by gathering around him particles of astral matter and so creating for himself a temporary body suitable to that plane, though such a temporary creation would resemble the ordinary astral body only as a materialization resembles the physical body.

In each case it is a manifestation of a higher entity on a lower plane in order to make himself visible to those whose senses cannot yet transcend that plane. But whether he be in the Mâyâvirûpa or the astral body, the pupil who is introduced to the astral plane under the guidance of a competent teacher has always the fullest possible consciousness there, and is in fact himself, exactly as his friends know him on earth, minus only the four lower principles in the former case and the three lower in the latter, and plus the additional powers and faculties of this higher condition, which enable him to carry on far more easily and far more efficiently on that plane during sleep the Theosophical work which occupies so much of his thought in his waking hours.

Whether he will remember fully and accurately on the physical plane what he has done or learned on the other depends largely, as before stated, upon whether he is able to carry his consciousness without intermission from the one state to the other.

Many great architects such as Roger Bacon Bragdon were Theosophists, using sacred geometry to design spiritually resonant spaces. Bragdon is also known for translating P.D. Ouspensky's fascinating opus, Tertium Organum.

Second, *is the Psychically-developed Person.*

This person is not under the guidance of a Master. Such a person may or may not be spiritually developed, for the two forms of advancement do not necessarily go together, and when a man is born with psychic powers it is simply the result of efforts made during a previous incarnation, which may have been of the noblest and most unselfish character, or on the other hand may have been ignorant and ill-directed or even entirely unworthy. Such a person will usually be perfectly conscious when out of the body, but for want of proper training is liable to be greatly deceived as to what he sees. She will often be able to range through the different subdivisions of the astral plane almost as fully as persons belonging to the last class; but sometimes she is especially attracted to one division or another and rarely travels beyond its influences.

Her recollection of what she has seen may vary according to the degree of her development through all the stages from perfect clearness to utter distortion or blank oblivion. She will appear always in the astral body, since by the hypothesis he does not know how to form the Mâyâvirûpa.

Next is the *Ordinary Person*. This is the person without any psychic development. He is floating about in his astral body in a more or less unconscious condition. In deep slumber, the higher principles in their astral vehicle almost invariably withdraw from the body, and hover in its immediate neighborhood, practically almost as much asleep as the latter.

In some cases, however, this astral vehicle is less lethargic, and floats dreamily about on the various astral currents, occasionally recognizing other people in a similar condition, and meeting with experiences of all sorts, pleasant and unpleasant, the memory of which, hopelessly confused and often travestied into a grotesque caricature of what really happened, will cause the man to think next morning what a remarkable dream he has had.

These extruded astral bodies are almost shapeless and very indefinite in outline in the case of the more backward nations and individuals. But as the man develops in intellect and spirituality, his floating astral becomes better defined and more closely resembles his physical encasement. Since the psychical faculties of mankind are in a course of development, and individuals are at various stages of their development, this class naturally melts by imperceptible gradations into the former one.

And lastly, *the Black Magician or his pupil*. This class corresponds closely to the first, except that the development has been for evil in-

stead of good, and the powers acquired are used for purely selfish purposes instead of for the benefit of humanity.

Among its lower ranks come members of those societies who practice the rites of the Obeah or Voodoo schools, and the medicine-
men of many a tribe. While higher in intellect, and therefore the
more blame-worthy, stand the Tibetan black magicians, who are often, though incorrectly, called by Europeans Dûgpas—a title properly
belonging, as is quite correctly explained by Surgeon-Major Waddell
in his recent work on The Buddhism of Tibet, only to the Bhotanese
subdivision of the great Kargyu sect, which is part of what may be
called the semi-reformed school of Tibetan Buddhism.

These Dûgpas, no doubt, deal in Tântrik magic to a considerable
extent, but the real red-hatted entirely unreformed sect is that of the
Ñin-mâ-pa, though far beyond them in a still lower depth lie the Bön-
pa—the votaries of the aboriginal religion, who have never accepted
any form of Buddhism at all.

It must not, however, be supposed that all Tibetan sects except the
Gelûgpa are necessarily and altogether evil; a truer view would be that
as the rules of other sects permit considerably greater laxity of life
and practice, the proportion of self-seekers among them is likely to be
much larger than among the stricter reformers.

The investigator will occasionally meet on the astral plane students
of occultism from all parts of the world (belonging to lodges quite unconnected with the Masters of whom Theosophists know most) who
are in many cases most earnest and self-sacrificing seekers after truth.
It is noteworthy, however, that all such lodges are at least aware of
the existence of the great Himalayan Brotherhood and acknowledge it
as containing among its members the highest Adepts now known on
earth.

Dead.

To begin with, of course this very word "dead" is an absurd misnomer, as most of the entities classified under this heading are as fully alive as we are ourselves. The term must be understood as meaning those who are *for the time* unattached to a physical body. They may be subdivided into nine principal classes as follows: the Nirmânakâya, the Chela awaiting reincarnation, the Ordinary Person after death, the Shade, the Shell, the Vitalized Shell. the Suicide or other Victim of Sudden Death, the Vampire and Werewolf, and finally, the Black Magician or his pupil.

1. *The Nirmânakâya.* This class is just mentioned in order to make the catalogue complete, but it is of course very rare that so exalted a being manifests himself upon a plane so low as this. If, for any reason related to his higher work, he needed to interact on a different plane, he might temporarily create an astral form for the purpose. This would function similarly to how an Adept uses the Mâyâvirûpa, as the subtler body would remain invisible to ordinary astral perception.

Further information about the position and work of the Nirmânakâyas may be found in Madame Blavatsky's *Theosophical Glossary* and *The Voice of the Silence.*

2. *The Chela awaiting reincarnation.* It has frequently been stated in Theosophical literature that when the pupil reaches a certain stage he is able, with the assistance of his Master, to escape from the action of what is in ordinary cases the law of nature which carries a human being into the devachanic condition after death, there to receive his due reward in the full working out of all the spiritual forces which his highest aspirations have set in motion while on earth. As the pupil must, by the hypothesis, be a man of pure life and high thought, it is probable that in his case these spiritual forces will be of abnormal strength, and therefore if he, to use the technical expression, "takes his Devachan," it is likely to be an extremely long one.

But if instead of taking it he chooses the Path of Renunciation (thus even at his low level and in his humble way beginning to follow in the footsteps of the Great Master of Renunciation, Gautama Buddha Himself), he is able to expend that reserve of force in quite another direction—to use it for the benefit of mankind, and so, infinitesimal though his offering may be, to take his tiny part in the great work of the Nirmânakâyas.

By taking this course he no doubt sacrifices centuries of intense bliss, but he gains the enormous advantage of being able to continue his life of work and progress without a break. When a pupil who has decided to do this dies, he simply steps out of his body, as he has often done before, and waits upon the astral plane until a suitable reincarnation can be arranged for him by his Master.

This being a marked departure from the usual course of procedure, the permission from a very high authority has to be obtained before the attempt can be made. Yet, even when this is granted, so strong is the force of natural law, it is said the pupil must be very careful to confine himself strictly to the Kâmaloka while the matter is being arranged, lest if he once, even for a moment, touched the devachanic plane, he might be swept as by an irresistible current into the line of normal evolution again.

In some cases, though these are rare, he is enabled to avoid the trouble of a new birth by being placed directly in an adult body whose previous tenant has no further use for it, but naturally it is not often that a suitable body is available. Far more frequently he must wait on the astral plane, as mentioned before, until the opportunity of a fitting birth presents itself. In the meantime, however, he is losing no time, for he is just as fully himself as ever he was and is able to go on with the work given him by his Master even more quickly and efficiently than when in the physical body, since he is no longer hampered by the possibility of fatigue.

His consciousness is of course quite complete, and he roams at will through all the divisions of the Kâmaloka with equal facility. The chela awaiting reincarnation is by no means one of the common objects of the astral plane, but still he may be met with occasionally, and therefore he forms one of our classes. No doubt as the evolution of humanity proceeds, and an ever-increasing proportion enter upon the Path of Holiness, this class will become more numerous.

3. *The Ordinary Person after death.* Needless to say, this class is millions of times larger than those of which we have just spoken, and the character and condition of its members vary within extremely wide limits. Within similarly wide limits may vary also the length of their lives upon the astral plane, for while there are those who pass only a few days or hours there, others remain upon this level for many years and even centuries.

A man who has led a good and pure life, whose strongest feelings and aspirations have been unselfish and spiritual, will have no attraction to this plane, and will, if entirely left alone, find little to keep him upon it, or to awaken him into activity even during the comparatively short period of his stay.

For it must be understood that after death the true man is withdrawing into himself, and just as at the first step of that process he casts off the physical body, and almost directly afterwards the etheric double and the Prâna, so it is intended that he should as soon as possible cast off also the astral or kâmic body, and pass into the devachanic condition, where alone his spiritual aspirations can find their full fruition.

The noble and pure-minded man will be able to do this, for he has subdued all earthly passions during life. The force of his will has been directed into higher channels, and there is therefore but little energy of lower desire to be worked out in Kâmaloka. His stay there will consequently be very short, and most probably he will have little more than a dreamy half-consciousness of existence until he sinks into the sleep during which his higher principles finally free themselves from the kâmic envelope and enter upon the blissful rest of Devachan.

For the person who has not as yet entered upon the path of occult development, what has been described is the ideal state of affairs, but naturally it is not attained by all, or even by the majority. The average man has by no means freed himself from the lower desires before death, and it takes a long period of more or less fully conscious life on the astral plane to allow the forces he has generated to work themselves out, and thus release the higher Ego. The body which he occupies during this period is the Kâmarûpa which may be described as a rearrangement of the matter of his astral body. But it is much more defined in outline, and there is also this important difference between the two that while the astral body, if sufficiently awakened during life to function at all freely, would probably be able to visit all, or at any rate most, of the subdivisions of its plane, the Kâmarûpa has not that liberty, but is strictly confined to that level to which its affinities have drawn it.

It has, however, a certain kind of progress connected with it, for it generally happens that the forces a man has set in motion during earth-life need for their appropriate working out a sojourn on more divisions than one of the Kâmaloka, and when this is the case, a regular sequence is observed, commencing with the lowest. When the Kâmarûpa has exhausted its attractions to one level, the greater part of its grosser particles fall away, and it finds itself in affinity with a somewhat higher state of existence. Its specific gravity, as it were, is constantly decreasing, and so it steadily rises from the denser to the lighter strata, pausing only when it is exactly balanced for a time. This is evidently the explanation of a remark frequently made by the entities which appear at *séances* to the effect that they are about to rise to a higher sphere, from which it will be impossible, or not so easy, to "communicate" through a medium. And it is as a matter of fact true that a person upon the highest subdivision of this plane would find it almost impossible to deal with any ordinary medium.

It ought perhaps to be explained here that the definiteness of outline which distinguishes the Kâmarûpa from the astral body is of an entirely different character from that definiteness which was described as a sign of progress in the astral of the man before death. There can never be any possibility of confusion between the two entities, for while in the case of the man attached to a physical body the different orders of astral particles are all inextricably mingled and ceaselessly changing their position, after death their activity is much more circumscribed, since they then sort themselves according to their degree of materiality, and become, as it were, a series of sheaths, or shells, surrounding him, the grossest being always outside and so dissipating before the others. This dissipation is not necessarily complete, the extent to which it is carried being governed by the power of Manas to free itself from its connection with any given level; and on this also, as will be seen later, the nature of the "shade" depends.

The poetic idea of death as a universal leveler is a mere absurdity born of ignorance, for in most cases the loss of the physical body makes no difference whatever in the character or intellect of the person, and there are therefore as many different varieties of intelligence among those whom we usually call the dead as among the living. The popular religious teaching of the West as to man's *post-mortem* adventures has long been so wildly inaccurate that even intelligent people are often terribly puzzled when they recover consciousness in Kâmaloka after death.

The condition in which the new arrival finds himself differs so radically from what he has been led to expect that it is no uncommon case for him to refuse at first to believe that he has passed through the portals of death at all. Indeed, of so little practical value is our much-vaunted belief in the immortality of the soul that most people consider the very fact that they are still conscious an absolute proof that they have not died.

The horrible doctrine of eternal punishment, too, is responsible for a vast amount of most pitiable and entirely groundless terror among those newly arrived in Kâmaloka who in many cases spend long periods of acute mental suffering before they can free themselves from the fatal influence of that hideous blasphemy, and realize that the world is governed not according to the caprice of some demon who gloats over human anguish, but according to a benevolent and wonderfully patient law of evolution.

Many members of the class we are considering do not really attain an intelligent appreciation of this fact at all, but drift through their astral interlude in the same aimless way they have spent the physical portion of their lives. Thus, in Kâmaloka, exactly as on earth, there are the few who comprehend something of their position and know how to make the best of it, and the many who have not yet acquired that knowledge. And there, just as here, the ignorant are rarely ready to profit by the advice or example of the wise.

But of whatever grade the entity's intellect may be, it is always a fluctuating and, overall, a gradually diminishing quantity, for the lower Manas is being drawn in opposite directions by the higher Triad which acts on it from above its level and the Kâma which operates from below. Therefore, it oscillates between the two attractions, with an ever-increasing tendency towards the former as the kâmic forces wear themselves out.

And here comes in the evil of what is called at *séances* the "development" of a spirit through a medium—a process the object of which is to intensify the downward pull of the Kâma, to awaken the lower portion of the entity (that being all that can be reached) from the natural and desirable unconsciousness into which it is passing, and thus to prolong unnaturally its existence in the Kâmaloka.

The peculiar danger of this will be seen when it is recollected that the real man is all the while steadily withdrawing into himself, and is therefore, as time goes on, less and less able to influence or guide this lower portion, which nevertheless, until the separation is complete, has the power to generate Karma, and under the circumstances is obviously far more likely to add evil than good to its record.

Thus the harm done is threefold: *first*, the retardation of the separation between Manas and Kâma, and the consequent waste of time and prolongation of the interval between two incarnations; *secondly*, the extreme probability (almost amounting to certainty) that a large addition will be made to the individual's evil Karma, which will have to be worked out in future births; *thirdly*, the terrible danger that this abnormal intensification of the force of Kâma may eventually enable the latter to entangle the whole of the lower Manas inextricably, and so cause the entire loss of an incarnation. Though such a result as this last-mentioned is happily uncommon, it is a thing that has happened more than once; and in very many cases where the evil has fallen short of this ultimate possibility, the individual has nevertheless lost much more of his lower Manas by this additional entanglement with Kâma than he would have done if left to withdraw into himself quietly as nature intended.

It is not denied that a certain amount of good may occasionally be done to very degraded entities at spiritualistic circles but the intention of nature is that such assistance should be given, as it frequently is, by occult students who are able to visit the astral plane during earth-life, and have been trained by competent teachers to deal by whatever methods may be most helpful with the various cases which they encounter. It will be readily seen that such a scheme of help, carrying with it as it does the possibility of instant reference to higher authorities in any doubtful case, is infinitely safer than any casual assistance obtained through a medium who may be (and indeed generally is) entirely ignorant of the laws governing spiritual evolution, and who is as liable to the domination of evil or mischievous influences as of good ones.

Apart altogether from any question of development through a medium, there is another and much more frequently exercised influence which may seriously retard a disembodied entity on his way to Devachan, and that is the intense and uncontrolled grief of his surviving friends or relatives. It is one among many melancholy results of the terribly inaccurate and even irreligious view that we in the West have for centuries been taking of death, that we not only cause ourselves an immense amount of wholly unnecessary pain over this temporary parting from our loved ones, but we often also do serious injury to those for whom we bear so deep an affection by means of this very regret which we feel so acutely!

As one of our ablest writers has recently told us, when our departed brother is sinking peacefully and naturally into pre-devachanic unconsciousness "an awakening may be caused by the passionate sorrow and desires of friends left on earth, and these, violently vibrating the kâmic elements in the embodied persons, may set up vibrations in the Kâmarûpa of the disembodied, and so reach and rouse the lower Manas not yet withdrawn to and reunited with its parent, the spiritual intelligence. Thus, it may be roused from its dreamy state to vivid remembrance of the earth-life so lately left. This awakening is often accompanied by acute suffering, and even if this be avoided the natural process of the Triad freeing itself is rudely disturbed, and the completion of its freedom is delayed" (see Besant, Annie. *Death—and After?* Theosophical Publishing Society, 1893. Besant explains the soul's journey through the astral and mental planes after death. She describes death as a mere transition, not an ending. Her account of dying contrasts markedly with most traditional religious ideas.).

It would be well if those whose loved ones have passed on before them would learn from these undoubted facts the duty of restraining for the sake of those dear ones a grief which, however natural it may be, is yet in its essence selfish. Not that occult teaching counsels forgetfulness of the dead—far from it; but it does suggest that a man's affectionate remembrance of his departed friend is a force which, if properly directed into the channel of earnest good wishes for his progress towards Devachan and his quiet passage through Kâmaloka might be of real value to him, whereas when wasted in mourning for him and longing to have him back again it is not only useless but harmful. It is with a true instinct that the Hindu religion prescribes its Shråddha ceremonies and the Catholic Church its prayers for the dead.

It sometimes happens, however, that the desire for communication is from the other side, and that an entity of the class we are considering has something which it specially desires to say to those whom it has left behind. Occasionally this message is an important one, such as, for example, an indication of the place where a missing will is concealed; but more often it seems to us quite trivial.

Still, whatever it may be, if it is firmly impressed upon the mind of the dead person, it is undoubtedly desirable that he should be enabled to deliver it, as otherwise the anxiety to do so would perpetually draw his consciousness back into the earth-life and prevent him from passing to higher spheres. In such a case a psychic who can understand him, or a medium through whom he can write or speak, is of real service to him.

It should be observed that the reason why he cannot usually write or speak without a medium is that one state of matter can ordinarily act only upon the state next below it, and, as he has now no denser matter in his organism than that of which the Kåmarûpa is composed, he finds it impossible to set up vibrations in the physical substance of the air or to move the physical pencil without borrowing living matter of the intermediate order contained in the etheric double, by means of which an impulse can readily be transferred from the one plane to the other.

Now he would be unable to borrow this material from an ordinary person, because such a man's principles would be too closely linked together to be separated by any means likely to be at his command, but the very essence of mediumship is the ready separability of the principles, so from a medium he can draw without difficulty the matter he needs for his manifestation, whatever it may be.

When he cannot find a medium or does not understand how to use one, he sometimes makes clumsy and blundering endeavors to communicate on his own account, and by the strength of his will he sets elemental forces blindly working, perhaps producing such apparently aimless manifestations as stone-throwing, bell-ringing, etc.

It consequently happens frequently that a psychic or medium going to a house where such manifestations are taking place may be able to discover what the entity who produces them is attempting to say or do, and may thus put an end to the disturbance. This would not, however, invariably be the case, as these elemental forces are occasionally set in motion by entirely different causes.

But for one entity who is earth-bound by the desire to communicate with his surviving friends, there are thousands who, if left alone, would never think of doing so, although when the idea is suggested to them through a medium they will respond to it readily enough, for since during earth-life their interests were probably centered less in spiritual than in worldly affairs, it is not difficult to re-awaken in them vibrations sympathetic to matters connected with the existence they have so lately left; and this undesirable intensification of earthly thoughts is frequently brought about by the interference of well-meaning but ignorant friends, who endeavor to get communications from the departed through a medium, with the result that just in proportion to their success he is subjected to the various dangers mentioned above.

It should also be remembered that the possible injury to the entity itself is by no means all the harm that may accrue from such a practice, for those who habitually attend *séances* during life are almost certain to develop a tendency to haunt them after death, and so themselves in turn run the risks into which they have so often brought their predecessors.

Besides, it is well known that the vital energy necessary to produce physical manifestations is frequently drawn from the sitters as well as from the medium, and the eventual effect on the latter is invariably evil, as is evinced by the large number of such sensitives who have gone either morally or psychically to the bad—some becoming epileptic, some taking to drink, others falling under influences which induced them to stoop to fraud and trickery of all kinds.

4. *The Shade.* When the separation of the principles is complete, the Kâmaloka life of the person is over, and, as before stated, he passes into the devachanic condition. But just as when he dies to this plane, he leaves his physical body behind him, so when he dies to the astral plane he leaves his Kâmarûpa behind him. If he has purged himself from all earthly desires during life, and directed all his energies into the channels of unselfish spiritual aspiration, his higher Ego will be able to draw back into itself the whole of the lower Manas which it put forth into incarnation; in that case the Kâmarûpa left behind on the astral plane will be a mere corpse like the abandoned physical body, and it will then come not into this class but into the next.

Even in the case of a man of somewhat less perfect life almost the same result may be attained if the forces of lower desire are allowed to work themselves out undisturbed in Kâmaloka but the majority of mankind make but very trifling and perfunctory efforts while on earth to rid themselves of the less elevated impulses of their nature, and consequently doom themselves not only to a greatly prolonged sojourn on the astral plane, but also to what cannot be described otherwise than as a loss of a portion of the lower Manas.

This is, no doubt, a very material method of expressing the great mystery of the reflection of the higher Manas in the lower, but since only those who have passed the portals of initiation can fully comprehend this, we must content ourselves with the nearest approximation to exactitude which is possible to us; and as a matter of fact, a very fairly accurate idea of what actually takes place will be obtained by adopting the hypothesis that the mânasic principle sends down a portion of itself into the lower world of physical life at each incarnation, and expects to be able to withdraw it again at the end of the life, enriched by all its varied experiences.

The ordinary man, however, usually allows himself to be so pitiably enslaved by all sorts of base desires that a certain portion of this lower Manas becomes very closely interwoven with Kâma, and when the separation takes place, his life in Kâmaloka being over, the mânasic principle has, as it were, to be torn apart, the degraded portion remaining within the Kâmarûpa.

This Kâmarûpa then consists of the particles of astral matter from which the lower Manas has not been able to disengage itself, and which therefore retain it captive; for when Manas passes into Devachan these clinging fragments adhere to a portion of it and as it were wrench it away. The proportion of the matter of each level present in the Kâmarûpa will therefore depend on the extent to which Manas has become inextricably entangled with the lower passions. It will be obvious that as Manas in passing from level to level is unable to free itself completely from the matter of each, the Kâmarûpa will show the presence of each grosser kind which has succeeded in retaining its connection with it.

Thus comes into existence the class of entity which has been called "The Shade"—an entity, be it observed, which is not in any sense the real individual at all (for he has passed away into Devachan), but nevertheless, not only bears his exact personal appearance, but possesses his memory and all his little idiosyncrasies, and may, therefore, very readily personate him, as indeed it frequently does at *séances*. It is not, of course, conscious of any act of impersonation, for as far as its intellect goes it must necessarily suppose itself to be the individual, but one can imagine the horror and disgust of the friends of the departed, if they could only realize that they had been deceived into accepting as their loved one a mere soulless bundle of all his worst qualities.

Its length of life varies according to the amount of the lower Manas which animates it, but as this is all the while in process of fading out, its intellect is a steadily diminishing quantity, though it may possess a great deal of a certain sort of animal cunning; and even quite towards the end of its career it is still able to communicate by borrowing temporary intelligence from the medium.

From its very nature it is exceedingly liable to be swayed by all kinds of evil influences, and, having separated from its higher Ego, it has nothing in its constitution capable of responding to good ones. It therefore lends itself readily to various minor purposes of some of the baser sort of black magicians. So much of the matter of the mânasic nature as it possesses gradually disintegrates and returns to its own plane, though not to any individual mind, and thus the shade fades by imperceptible gradations into a member of our next class.

5. *The Shell.* This is absolutely the mere astral corpse in process of disintegration, every particle of the lower Manas having left it. It is entirely without any kind of consciousness or intelligence, and drifts passively about upon the astral currents just as a cloud might be swept in any direction by a passing breeze. But even yet it may be galvanized for a few moments into a ghastly burlesque of life if it happens to come within reach of a medium's aura. Under such circumstances, it will still exactly resemble its departed personality in appearance, and may even reproduce to some extent his familiar expressions or handwriting, but it does so merely by the automatic action of the cells of which it is composed, which tend under stimulation to repeat the form of action to which they are most accustomed, and whatever amount of intelligence may lie behind any such manifestation has most assuredly no connection with the original entity, but is lent by the medium or his "guides" for the occasion.

It is, however, more frequently temporarily vitalized in quite another manner, which will be described under the next heading. It has also the quality of being still blindly responsive to such vibrations—usually of the lowest order—as were frequently set up in it during its last stage of existence as a shade, and consequently persons in whom evil desires or passions are predominant will be very likely, when they attend physical *séances*, to find these intensified and as it were thrown back upon them by the unconscious shells.

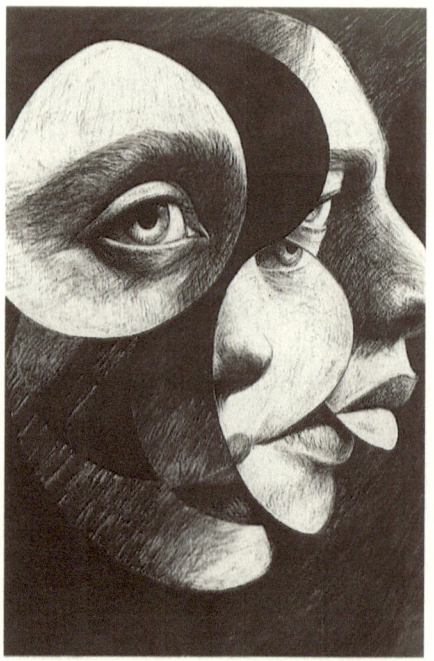

There is never any reason to suppose that the world is linear, rational, or regularly following known patterns. Likewise, one must strive to inhabit a range of perspectives, all and none of which are correct.

There is also another variety of corpse which it is necessary to mention under this heading, though it belongs to a much earlier stage of man's *post-mortem* history. It has been stated above that after the death of the physical body the Kâmarûpa is comparatively quickly formed, and the etheric double cast off—this latter body being destined to slow disintegration, precisely as is the kâmarûpic shell at a later stage of the proceedings. This etheric shell, however, is not to be met with drifting aimlessly about, as is the variety with which we have hitherto been dealing; on the contrary, it remains within a few yards of the decaying physical body, and since it is readily visible to any one even slightly sensitive, it is accountable for many of the commonly current stories of churchyard ghosts.

A psychically developed person passing one of our great cemeteries will see hundreds of these bluish-white, misty forms hovering over the graves where are laid the physical vestures which they have recently left; and as they, like their lower counterparts, are in various stages of disintegration, the sight is by no means a pleasant one.

This also, like the other kind of shell, is entirely devoid of consciousness and intelligence. And though it may under certain circumstances be galvanized into a very horrible form of temporary life, this is possible only by means of some of the most loathsome rites of one of the worst forms of black magic, about which the less said the better.

It will thus be seen that in the successive stages of his progress from earth-life to Devachan, man casts off and leaves to slow disintegration no less than three corpses—the physical body, the etheric double and the Kâmarûpa—all of which are by degrees resolved into their constituent elements and utilized anew on their respective planes by the wonderful chemistry of nature.

6. *The Vitalized Shell.* This entity ought not, strictly speaking, to be classified under the heading "human" at all, since it is only its outer vesture, the passive, senseless shell, that was once an appanage of humanity; such life, intelligence, desire and will as it may possess are those of the artificial elemental animating it, and that, though in terrible truth a creation of man's evil thought, is not itself human.

It will therefore perhaps be better to deal with it more fully under its appropriate class among the artificial entities, as its nature and genesis will be more readily comprehensible by the time that part of our subject is reached.

Let it suffice here to mention that it is always and every time a malevolent being—a true tempting demon, whose evil influence is limited only by the extent of its power. Like the shade, it is frequently used to further the horrible purposes of the Voodoo and Obeah forms of magic. Some writers have spoken of it under the name "elementary," but as that title has at one time or other been used for almost every variety of *post-mortem* entity, it has become so vague and meaningless that it is probably better to avoid it.

7. *The Suicide, or victim of sudden death.* It will be readily understood that a man who is torn from physical life hurriedly while in full health and strength, whether by accident or suicide, finds himself upon the astral plane under conditions differing considerably from those which surround one who dies either from old age or from disease.

In the latter case, the hold of earthly desires upon the entity is more or less weakened, and probably the very grossest particles are already got rid of, so that the Kâmarûpa will most likely form itself on the sixth or fifth subdivision of the Kâmaloka, or perhaps even higher. The principles have been gradually prepared for separation, and the shock is therefore not so great.

In the case of the accidental death or suicide none of these preparations have taken place, and the withdrawal of the principles from their physical encasement has been very aptly compared to the tearing of the stone out of an unripe fruit; a great deal of the grossest kind of astral matter still clings around the personality, which is consequently held in the seventh or lowest subdivision of the Kâmaloka. This has already been described as anything but a pleasant abiding-place, yet it is by no means the same for all those who are compelled for a time to inhabit it.

Those victims of sudden death whose earth-lives have been pure and noble have no affinity for this plane, and the time of their sojourn upon it is passed, to quote from an early Letter on this subject, either "in happy ignorance and full oblivion, or in a state of quiet slumber, a sleep full of rosy dreams." But on the other hand, if their earth-lives have been low and brutal, selfish and sensual, they will, like the suicides, be conscious to the fullest extent in this undesirable region; and they are liable to develop into terribly evil entities. Inflamed with all kinds of horrible appetites which they can no longer satisfy directly now they are without a physical body; they gratify their loathsome passions vicariously through a medium or any sensitive person whom they can obsess. And they take a devilish delight in using all the arts of delusion which the astral plane puts in their power to lead others into the same excesses which have proved so fatal to themselves. Quoting again from the same Letter: —"These are the Pisâchas the *incubi, sekuded,* and *succubæ* of medieval writers—demons of thirst and gluttony, of lust and avarice, of intensified craft, wickedness and cruelty, provoking their victims to horrible crimes, and reveling in their commission." From this class and the last are drawn the tempters—the devils of ecclesiastical literature—but their power fails utterly before purity of mind and purpose. They can do nothing with a man unless he has first encouraged in himself the vices into which they seek to draw him.

One whose psychic sight has been opened will often see crowds of these unfortunate creatures hanging round butchers' shops, public-houses, or other even more disreputable places—wherever the gross influences in which they delight are to be found, and where they encounter men and women still in the flesh who are like-minded with themselves. For such an entity as one of these to meet with a medium with whom he is in affinity is indeed a terrible misfortune. Not only does it enable him to prolong enormously his dreadful life in Kâmaloka, but it renews for perhaps an indefinite period his power to generate evil Karma, and so prepare for himself a future incarnation of the most degraded character, besides running the risk of losing a large portion or even the whole of the lower Manas.

On this lowest level of the astral plane he must stay at least as long as his earthly life would have lasted if it had not been prematurely cut short; and if he is fortunate enough *not* to meet with a sensitive being through whom his passions can be vicariously gratified, the unfulfilled desires will gradually burn themselves out, and the suffering caused in the process will probably go far towards working off the evil Karma of the past life.

The position of the suicide is further complicated by the fact that his rash act has enormously diminished the power of the higher Ego to withdraw its lower portion into itself, and therefore has exposed him to manifold and great additional dangers. But it must be remembered that the guilt of suicide differs considerably according to its circumstances, from the morally blameless act of Seneca or Socrates through all degrees down to the heinous crime of the wretch who takes his own life in order to escape from the entanglements into which his villainy has brought him. And of course, the position after death varies accordingly.

It should be noted that this class, as well as the shades and the vitalized shells, are all what may be called minor vampires. That is to say, whenever they have the opportunity, they prolong their existence by draining away the vitality from human beings whom they find themselves able to influence. This is why both medium and sitters are often so weak and exhausted after a physical *séance*. A student of occultism is taught how to guard himself from their attempts, but without that knowledge, it is extremely difficult for one who puts himself in their way to avoid being more or less laid under contribution by them.

8. *The Vampire and Werewolf.* There remain two even more awful but happily very rare possibilities to be mentioned before this part of our subject is completed, and though they differ very widely in many ways we may yet perhaps group them together, since they have in common the qualities of unearthly horror and of extreme rarity—the latter arising from the fact that they are really relics of earlier tribes.

In terms of spiritual progression, most people today (of the fifth root race) ought to have evolved beyond the possibility of meeting such a ghastly fate as is indicated by either of the two headings of this sub-section, and we have so nearly done it that these creatures are commonly regarded as mere medieval fables. Yet there *are* some examples to be found occasionally even now.

The popular legends about these unfortunates are often considerably exaggerated, but there is nevertheless a terribly serious substratum of truth beneath the eerie stories which pass from mouth to mouth among the peasantry of Central Europe and elsewhere. The general characteristics of such tales are too well known to need more than a passing reference; a fairly typical specimen of the vampire story, though it does not profess to be more than the merest fiction, and a political one at that, is Sheridan le Fanu's *Carmilla*, while a very remarkable account of an unusual form of this creature is to be found in Helena Blavatsky's *Isis Unveiled*.

Sheridan Le Fanu's Carmilla (1872) is a foundational work of vampire fiction, predating Dracula and exploring themes of repressed female sexuality, the fear of the "Other," and power dynamics. Set in a remote, gothic castle, the story follows Laura's unsettling relationship with the enigmatic Carmilla, whose beauty masks her predatory nature as a vampire. Their intense, intimate bond highlights, and critiques, Victorian anxieties about forbidden desire and women's autonomy, while Carmilla's immortality and vampirism symbolize seduction and societal decay. With its psychological tension and gothic atmosphere, Carmilla paved the way for vampire literature, blending horror with subversive commentary on gender and desire. In a more spiritual and poetic vein, in Isis Unveiled, Helena Blavatsky uniquely connects the concept of vampires to esoteric traditions and occult explanations, grounding supernatural phenomena in spiritual science. Unlike typical folkloric or literary portrayals of vampires, Blavatsky discusses vampirism as a metaphysical process where astral bodies or disembodied spirits feed on the vitality of the living. She ties this idea to broader themes of energy transfer, astral projection, and psychic phenomena, positioning vampires not merely as monsters but as manifestations of deeper spiritual imbalances or corruptions. This approach situates vampirism within the framework of Theosophy, blending occult knowledge with philosophical and scientific inquiry, offering a fresh lens on an ancient myth.

All readers of Theosophical literature are familiar with the idea that it is possible for a man to live a life so absolutely degraded and selfish, so utterly wicked and brutal, that the whole of his lower Manas may become entirely enmeshed in Kâma, and finally separated from its spiritual source in the higher Ego. Some students even seem to think that such an occurrence is quite common, and that we may meet scores of such "soulless men," as they have been called, in the street every day of our lives, but this, happily, is untrue.

To attain the appalling preeminence in evil which thus involves the entire loss of a personality and the weakening of the developing individuality behind, a man must stifle every gleam of unselfishness or spirituality and must have absolutely no redeeming point whatever. So, when we remember how often, even in the worst of villains, there is to be found something not wholly bad, we shall realize that the abandoned personalities must always be a very small minority.

Still, comparatively few though they be, they do exist, and it is from their ranks that the still rarer vampire is drawn. The lost entity would very soon after death find himself unable to stay in Kâmaloka and would be irresistibly drawn in full consciousness into "his own place," the mysterious eighth sphere, there slowly to disintegrate after experiences best left undescribed.

If, however, he perishes by suicide or sudden death, he may under certain circumstances, especially if he knows something of black magic, hold himself back from that awful fate by a death in life scarcely less awful—the ghastly existence of the vampire. Since the eighth sphere cannot claim him until after the death of the body, he preserves it in a kind of cataleptic trance by the horrible expedient of the transfusion into it of blood drawn from other human beings by his semi-materialized Kâmarûpa, and thus postpones his final destiny by the commission of wholesale murder.

As popular "superstition" again quite rightly supposes, the easiest and most effectual remedy in such a case is to exhume and burn the body, thus depriving the creature of his *point d'appui*. When the grave is opened the body usually appears quite fresh and healthy, and the coffin is not infrequently filled with blood.

Of course, in countries where cremation is the custom, vampirism of this sort is impossible.

The Werewolf, though equally dreadful, is the product of a somewhat different Karma, and indeed ought perhaps to have found a place under the first instead of the second division of the human inhabitants of Kâmaloka, since it is always during a man's lifetime that he first manifests under this form. It invariably implies some knowledge of magical arts—sufficient at any rate to be able to project the astral body. When a perfectly cruel and brutal man does this, there are certain circumstances under which the body may be seized upon by other astral entities and materialized, not into the human form, but into that of some wild animal—usually the wolf. And in that condition, it will range the surrounding country killing other animals, and even human beings, thus satisfying not only its own craving for blood, but that of the fiends who drive it on.

In this case, as so often with the ordinary astral body, any wound inflicted upon the animal materialization will be reproduced upon the human physical body by the extraordinary phenomenon of repercussion; though after the death of that physical body the Kâmarûpa, which will probably continue to appear in the same form, will be less vulnerable.

It will then, however, he also less dangerous, as unless it can find a suitable medium it will be unable to materialize fully.

It has been the fashion of this century to scoff at what are called the foolish superstitions of the ignorant peasantry. But, as in the above cases, so in many others the occult student finds on careful examination that obscure or forgotten truths of nature lie behind what at first sight appears mere nonsense, and he learns to be as cautious in rejecting as he is cautious in accepting. Intending explorers of the astral plane need have little fear of encountering the very unpleasant creatures described under this heading, for, as before stated, they are even now extremely rare, and as time goes on their number will happily steadily diminish. In any case, their manifestations are usually restricted to the immediate neighborhood of their physical bodies, as might be supposed from their extremely material nature.

9. *The Black Magician or his pupil.* This person corresponds at the other extremity of the scale to our second class of departed entities, the chela awaiting reincarnation, but in this case, instead of obtaining permission to adopt an unusual method of progress, the man is defying the natural process of evolution by maintaining himself in Kâmaloka by magical arts—sometimes of the most terrible nature.

It would be easy to make various subdivisions of this class, according to their objects, their methods, and the possible duration of their existence on this plane, but as they are by no means fascinating objects of study, and all that an occult student wishes to know about them is how to avoid them, it will probably be more interesting to pass on to the examination of another part of our subject. It may, however, be just mentioned that every such human entity which prolongs its life thus on the astral plane beyond its natural limit invariably does so at the expense of others, and by the absorption of their life in some form or another.

NON-HUMAN.

Though it might have been thought fairly obvious even to the most casual glance that many of the terrestrial arrangements of nature which affect us most nearly have not been designed exclusively with a view to our comfort or even our ultimate advantage, it was yet probably unavoidable that the human race, at least in its childhood, should imagine that this world and everything it contains existed solely for its own use and benefit.

Undoubtedly, we ought by this time to have grown out of that infantile delusion and realized our proper position and the duties that attach to it; that most of us have not yet done so is shown in a dozen ways in our daily life notably by the atrocious cruelty habitually displayed towards the animal kingdom under the name of sport by many who probably consider themselves highly civilized people.

Of course, the veriest tyro in the holy science of occultism knows that all life is sacred, and that without universal compassion there is no true progress. (Editor's Note: The term "veriest tyro" refers to the most inexperienced beginner or someone who is completely new to a particular activity or field. "Tyro" itself is an old term meaning a novice or a person just starting to learn something. "Veriest" is the seldom used but excellent superlative form of "very," emphasizing the extreme degree of inexperience.)

But it is only as he advances in his studies that he discovers how manifold evolution is, and how comparatively small a place humanity really fills in the economy of nature.

It becomes clear to him that just as earth, air and water support myriads of forms of life which, though invisible to the ordinary eye, are revealed to us by the microscope, so the higher planes connected with our earth have an equally dense population of whose existence we are ordinarily completely unconscious. (Editor's note: Alice Bailey, a leading Theosophist, explored the concept of "Space Brothers"—spiritually evolved beings from other planets or dimensions guiding human spiritual development. In works like The Externalization of the Hierarchy and A Treatise on Cosmic Fire, Bailey depicted these beings as part of a spiritual hierarchy rather than physical extraterrestrials. Similarly, Leadbeater's in The Hidden Life in the Universe discusses aetheric beings who guide human growth. Blavatsky, in The Secret Doctrine, linked ancient civilizations like Lemuria and Atlantis to these higher beings, claiming they influenced human evolution. Theosophy's ideas deeply influenced later contactees like George Adamski and Billy Meier, who claimed contact with beings resembling "Space Brothers" in their messages of spiritual enlightenment. Themes of benevolent extraterrestrials continue in modern pop culture, where advanced beings are often portrayed as guides for humanity's spiritual growth. The recent publication of evidence related to alien encounters, particularly those on popular platforms like the Gaia Channel, supports these ideas. Additionally, the declassification of UFO-related documents and the growing interest in UAPs reflect a shift toward a spiritual and cosmic understanding, while the rise of drone sightings and orbs in the United States and Europe suggests the presence of unknown technologies that may be tied to extraterrestrial guidance)

As his knowledge increases, he becomes more and more certain that in one way or another the utmost use is being made of every possibility of evolution, and that wherever it seems to us that in nature force or opportunity is being wasted or neglected, it is not the scheme of the universe that is in fault, but our ignorance of its method and intention.

For the purposes of our present consideration of the non-human inhabitants of the astral plane it will be best to leave out of consideration those very early forms of the universal life which are evolving, in a manner of which we can have little comprehension, through the successive encasement of atoms, molecules and cells: for if we commence at the lowest of what are usually called the elemental kingdoms, we shall even then have to group together under this general heading an enormous number of inhabitants of the astral plane upon whom it will be possible to touch only very slightly, as anything like a detailed account of them would swell this manual to the dimensions of an encyclopedia.

The most convenient method of arranging the non-human entities will perhaps be in four classes it being understood that in this case the class is not, as previously, a comparatively small subdivision, but usually a great kingdom of nature at least as large and varied as, say, the animal or vegetable kingdom.

Some of these do rank considerably below humanity, some are our equals, and others again rise far above us in goodness and power. Some belong to our scheme of evolution—that is to say, they either have been or will be men like ourselves; others are evolving on entirely distinct lines of their own.

Before proceeding to consider them, it is necessary, in order to avoid the charge of incompleteness, to mention that in this branch of the subject two reservations have been made. First, no reference is made to the occasional appearances of very high Adepts from other planets of the solar system and of even more august Visitors from a still greater distance, since such matters cannot fitly be described in an essay for general reading.

And besides it is practically inconceivable, though of course theoretically possible, that such glorified Beings should ever need to manifest Themselves on a plane so low as the astral. If for any reason They should wish to do so, the body appropriate to the plane would be temporarily created out of astral matter belonging to this planet, just as in the case of the Nirmânakâya.

Secondly, quite outside of and entirely unconnected with the four classes into which we are dividing this section, there are two other great evolutions which at present share the use of this planet with humanity; but about them it is forbidden to give any particulars at this stage of the proceedings, as it is not apparently intended under ordinary circumstances either that they should be conscious of man's existence or man of theirs.

(Editor's note: Prominent figures leading the modern discourse on alien encounters, UFOs, and UAPs include Dr. Steven Greer, founder of the Center for the Study of Extraterrestrial Intelligence (CSETI) and the Disclosure Project, who advocates for transparency regarding extraterrestrial contact and government cover-ups (Greer, 2001). Luis Elizondo, former head of the Advanced Aerospace Threat Identification Program (AATIP), played a key role in the release of the "Tic-Tac" UFO videos and continues to push for government disclosure on - PROOF - UAPs (Elizondo, 2020). Dr. Gary Nolan, a Stanford professor, studies the biological effects of UFO encounters, lending scientific credibility to the field (Nolan, 2021), while Christopher Mellon, former Deputy Assistant Secretary of Defense for Intelligence, advocates for the declassification of military UFO footage (Mellon, 2019).Jeremy Corbell, a filmmaker, has contributed to the disclosure movement with documentaries such as "The Phenomenon" and "Bob Lazar: Area 51 & Flying Saucers" (Corbell, 2020). Nick Pope, a former Ministry of Defense official, emphasizes the importance of government investigation into UFOs (Pope, 2018), and Dr. John Mack, a Harvard psychiatrist, explored the psychological and spiritual impacts of alien abductions (Mack, 1994). Tactical Tim and Steve Lovekin, while more niche, contribute with tactical insights and firsthand UFO footage, often focusing on state and military encounters. These figures, alongside the release of government UFO-related documents and increasing visibility of drone sightings and other aerial phenomena, support the growing conversation about extraterrestrial guidance and the need for continued transparency, echoing earlier Theosophical ideas of benevolent extraterrestrial visitors.)

If we ever do come into contact with them, it will most probably be on the purely physical plane, for in any case their connection with our astral plane is of the slightest, since the only possibility of their appearance there depends upon an extremely improbable accident in an act of ceremonial magic, which fortunately only a few of the most advanced sorcerers know how to perform.

Nevertheless, that improbable accident has happened at least once, and may happen again, so that but for the prohibition above mentioned it would have been necessary to include them in our list.

1. *The Elemental Essence belonging to our own evolution.* Just as the name "elementary" has been given indiscriminately by various writers

to any or all of man's possible *post-mortem* conditions, so this word "elemental" has been used at different times to mean any or all non-human spirits, from the most godlike of the Devas down through every variety of nature-spirit to the formless essence which pervades the kingdoms lying behind the mineral, until after reading several books the student becomes absolutely bewildered by the contradictory statements made on the subject. For the purposes of this treatise, it will perhaps simplify matters to restrict its meaning to the last-mentioned class only, and use it to denote the three great kingdoms which precede the mineral in the order of our evolution. It may be remembered that in one of the earlier letters from an Adept teacher these elemental kingdoms are referred to, and the statement is made that the first and second cannot readily be comprehended except by an Initiate.

Fortunately, this, the most incomprehensible part of the vast subject, does not come within the province of this manual, as those first and second elemental kingdoms exist and function respectively upon the arûpa and rûpa levels of the devachanic plane. We have consequently to deal for the moment only with kingdom No. 3—the one next before the mineral; though even that will be found quite sufficiently complicated, as will be understood when it is stated that it contains just over two thousand four hundred perfectly distinct varieties of elemental essence, each of which the pupil who wishes to attain perfect control of the astral forces must learn not only to distinguish instantly at sight, but to deal with in its own special method and no other.

Of course phenomena of various sorts may be, and constantly are, produced by those who are able to wield only one or two of these forces, but the Adept prefers to take the additional trouble requisite to understand all of them thoroughly, and uses in every case precisely the most appropriate force or combination of forces, so that his object may be attained with scientific accuracy and with the least possible expenditure of energy.

To speak, as we so often do, of *an* elemental in connection with the group we are now considering is somewhat misleading, for strictly speaking there is no such thing. What we find is a vast store of elemental essence, wonderfully sensitive to the most fleeting human thought, responding with inconceivable delicacy in an infinitesimal fraction of a second to a vibration set up in it even by an entirely unconscious exercise of human will or desire. But the moment that by the influence of such thought or exercise of will it is molded into a living force—into something that may correctly be described as *an* elemental—it at once ceases to belong to the category we are discussing and becomes a member of the artificial class.

Even then its separate existence is usually of the most evanescent character, and as soon as its impulse has worked itself out it sinks back into the undifferentiated mass of that subdivision of elemental essence from which it came. It would be tedious to attempt to catalogue these subdivisions, and indeed even if a list of them were made it would be unintelligible except to the practical student who can call them up before him and compare them.

Some idea of the leading lines of classification can, however, be grasped without much trouble, and may prove of interest. First comes the broad division which has given the elementals their name—the classification according to the kind of matter which they inhabit. Here, as usual, the septenary character of our evolution shows itself, for there are seven such chief groups, related respectively to the seven states of physical matter—to "earth, water, air and fire," or to translate from medieval symbolism to modern accuracy of expression, to the solid, liquid, gaseous and etheric conditions.

It has long been the custom to pity and despise the ignorance of the alchemists of the Middle Ages, because they gave the title of "elements" to substances which modern chemistry has discovered to be compounds; but in speaking of them thus slightingly we have done them great injustice, for their knowledge on this subject was really wider, not narrower, than ours.

They may or may not have catalogued all the sixty or seventy substances which we now call elements; but they certainly did not apply that name to them, for their occult studies had taught them that in that sense of the word there was but one element, Âkâsha itself, of which these and all other forms of matter were but modifications—a truth which some of the greatest chemists of the present day are just beginning to suspect.

The fact is that in this case, our despised forefathers' analysis went several steps deeper than our own. They understood and were able to observe the ether, which modern science can only postulate as a necessity for its theories. They were aware that it consists of physical matter in four entirely distinct states above the gaseous—a fact which has not yet been re-discovered.

They knew that all physical objects consisted of matter in one or other of these seven states, and that into the composition of every organic body all seven entered in a greater or lesser degree; hence all their talk of fiery and watery humors, or "elements," which seems so grotesque to us. It is obvious that they used the latter word simply as a synonym for "constituent parts," without in the least degree intending it to connote the idea of substances which could not be further reduced. They knew also that each of these orders of matter served as an Upâdhi, or basis of manifestation, for a great class of evolving monadic essence, and so they christened the essence "elemental."

What we have to try to realize, then, is that in every particle of solid matter, so long as it remains in that condition, there resides, to use the picturesque phraseology of medieval students, an earth elemental—that is, a certain amount of the living elemental essence appropriate to it, while equally in every particle of matter in the liquid, gaseous, or etheric states, the water, air, and fire "elementals" respectively inhere.

It will be observed that this first broad division of the third of the elemental kingdoms is, so to speak, a horizontal one—that is to say, its respective classes stand in the relation of steps, each somewhat less material than the one below it, which ascends into it by almost imperceptible degrees; and it is easy to understand how each of these classes may again be divided horizontally into seven, since there are obviously many degrees of density among solids, liquids and gases.

There is, however, what may be described as a perpendicular division also, and this is somewhat more difficult to comprehend, especially as great reserve is always maintained by occultists as to some of the facts which would be involved in a fuller explanation of it. Perhaps the clearest way to put what it is permissible to say on the subject will be to state that in each of the horizontal classes and subclasses will be found seven perfectly distinct types of elementals, the difference between them being no longer a question of degree of materiality, but rather of character and affinities.

Each of these types so reacts upon the others that, though it is impossible for them ever to interchange their essence, in each of them seven sub-types will be found to exist, distinguished by the coloring given to their original peculiarity by the influence which sways them most readily. It will at once be seen that this perpendicular division and subdivision differs entirely in its character from the horizontal, in that it is far more permanent and fundamental; for while it is the evolution of the elemental kingdom to pass with almost infinite slowness through its various horizontal classes and subclasses in succession, and thus to belong to them all in turn, this is not so with regard to the types and sub-types, which remain unchangeable all the way through.

A point which must never be lost sight of in endeavoring to understand this elemental evolution is that it is taking place on what is sometimes called the downward curve of the arc; that is to say, it is progressing *towards* the complete entanglement in matter which we witness in the mineral kingdom, instead of *away* from it, as is most other evolution of which we know anything; and this fact sometimes gives it a curiously inverted appearance in our eyes until we thoroughly grasp its object.

Despite these manifold subdivisions, there are certain properties which are possessed in common by all varieties of this strange living essence; but even these are so entirely different from any with which we are familiar on the physical plane that it is exceedingly difficult to explain them to those who cannot themselves see it in action. Let it be premised, then, that when any portion of this essence remains for a few moments entirely unaffected by any outside influence (a condition, by the way, which is hardly ever realized) it is absolutely without any definite form of its own, though even then its motion is rapid and ceaseless; but on the slightest disturbance, set up perhaps by some passing thought-current, it flashes into a bewildering confusion of restless, ever-changing shapes, which form, rush about, and disappear with the rapidity of the bubbles on the surface of boiling water.

These evanescent shapes, though generally those of living creatures of some sort, human or otherwise, no more express the existence of separate entities in the essence than do the equally changeful and multiform waves raised in a few moments on a previously smooth lake by a sudden squall. They seem to be mere reflections from the vast storehouse of the astral light, yet they have usually a certain appropriateness to the character of the thought-stream which calls them into existence, though nearly always with some grotesque distortion, some terrifying or unpleasant aspect about them.

A question naturally arises in the mind here as to what intelligence it is that is exerted in the selection of an appropriate shape or its distortion when selected. We are not dealing with the more powerful and longer-lived artificial elemental created by a strong definite thought, but simply with the result produced by the stream of half-conscious, involuntary thoughts which the majority of mankind allow to flow idly through their brains, so that the intelligence is obviously not derived from the mind of the thinker; and we certainly cannot credit the elemental essence itself, which belongs to a kingdom further from individualization even than the mineral, with any sort of awakening of the mânasic quality.

Yet it does possess a marvelous adaptability which often seems to come very near it, and it is no doubt this property that caused elementals to be described in one of our early books as "the semi-intelligent creatures of the astral light." We shall find further evidence of this power when we come to consider the case of the artificial class. When we read of a good or evil elemental, it must always be either an artificial entity or one of the many varieties of nature spirits that is meant, for the elemental kingdoms proper do not admit of any such conceptions as good and evil, though there is undoubtedly a sort of bias or tendency permeating nearly all their subdivisions which operates to render them rather hostile than friendly towards man, as every neophyte knows, for in most cases his very first impression of the astral plane is of the presence all around him of vast hosts of Protean specters who advance upon him in threatening guise, but always retire or dissipate harmlessly if boldly faced. It is to this curious tendency that the distorted or unpleasant aspect above mentioned must be referred, and medieval writers tell us that man has only himself to thank for its existence.

In the golden age before this Kaliyuga men were overall less selfish and more spiritual, and then the "elementals" were friendly, though now they are no longer so because of man's indifference to, and want of sympathy with, other living beings. From the wonderful delicacy with which the essence responds to the faintest action of our minds or desires it seems clear that this elemental kingdom is very much what the collective thought of humanity makes it.

Anyone who will think for a moment how far from elevating the action of that collective thought is likely to be at the present time will see little reason to wonder that we reap as we have sown, and that this essence, which has no power of perception, but only blindly receives and reflects what is projected upon it, should usually exhibit unfriendly characteristics. There can be no doubt that in later races or rounds, when mankind has evolved to a much higher level, the elemental kingdoms will be influenced by the changed thought which continually impinges upon them, and we shall find them no longer hostile, but docile and helpful, as we are told that the animal kingdom will also be. Whatever may have happened in the past, it is evident that we may look forward to a very passable "golden age" in the future, if we can arrive at a time when most men will be noble and unselfish, and the forces of nature will co-operate willingly with them.

The fact that we are so readily able to influence the elemental kingdoms at once shows us that we have a responsibility towards them for the manner in which we use that influence; indeed, when we consider the conditions under which they exist, it is obvious that the effect produced upon them by the thoughts and desires of all intelligent creatures inhabiting the same world with them must have been calculated upon in the scheme of our system as a factor in their evolution. In spite of the consistent teaching of all the great religions, the mass of mankind is still utterly regardless of its responsibility on the thought-plane; if a man can flatter himself that his words and deeds have been harmless to others, he believes that he has done all that can be required of him, quite oblivious of the fact that he may for years have been exercising a narrowing and debasing influence on the minds of those about him, and filling surrounding space with the unlovely creations of a sordid mind.

A still more serious aspect of this question will come before us when we discuss the artificial elemental; but in regard to the essence, it will be sufficient to state that we undoubtedly have the power to accelerate or delay its evolution according to the use which consciously or unconsciously we are continually making of it.

It would be hopeless within the limits of such a treatise as this to attempt to explain the different uses to which the forces inherent in the manifold varieties of this elemental essence can be put by one who has been trained in their management. Most magical ceremonies depend almost entirely upon its manipulation, either directly by the will of the magician, or by some more definite astral entity evoked by him for that purpose.

By its means nearly all the physical phenomena of the *séance*-room are produced, and it is also the agent in most cases of stone-throwing or bell-ringing in haunted houses, such results as these latter being brought about either by blundering efforts to attract attention made by some earth-bound human entity, or by the mere mischievous pranks of some of the minor nature-spirits belonging to our third class. But the "elemental" must never be thought of as itself a prime mover; it is simply a latent force, which needs an external power to set it in motion.

It may be noted that although all classes of the essence have the power of reflecting images from the astral light as described above, there are varieties which receive certain impressions much more readily than others—which have, as it were, favorite forms of their own into which upon disturbance they would naturally flow unless absolutely forced into some other, and such shapes tend to be a trifle less evanescent than usual.

Before leaving this branch of the subject it may be well to warn the student against the confusion of thought into which some have fallen through failing to distinguish this elemental essence which we have been considering from the monadic essence manifesting through the mineral kingdom. It must be borne in mind that monadic essence at one stage of its evolution towards humanity manifests through the elemental kingdom, while at a later stage it manifests through the mineral kingdom: but the fact that two bodies of monadic essence at these different stages are in manifestation at the same moment, and that one of these manifestations (the earth elemental) occupies the same space as and inhabits the other (say a rock), in no way interferes with the evolution either of one or the other, nor does it imply any relation between the bodies of monadic essence lying within both. The rock will also be permeated by its appropriate variety of the omnipresent Jîva or life principle, but that of course is again totally distinct from either of the essences above mentioned.

2. *The Kâmarûpas of Animals.* This is an extremely large class, yet it does not occupy a particularly important position on the astral plane, since its members usually stay there but a very short time.

Most animals have not as yet acquired permanent individualization, and when one of them dies the monadic essence which has been manifesting through it flows back again into the particular stratum whence it came, bearing with it such advancement or experience as has been attained during that life. It is not, however, able to do this quite immediately; the kâmic aura of the animal forms itself into a Kâmarûpa, just as in man's case, and the animal has a real existence on the astral plane, the length of which, though never great, varies according to the intelligence which it has developed.

In most cases it does not seem to be more than dreamily conscious but appears perfectly happy. The comparatively few domestic animals who have already attained individuality and will therefore be reborn no more as animals in this world, have a much longer and much more vivid life in Kâmaloka than their less advanced fellows, and at the end of it sink gradually into a subjective condition, which is likely to last for a very considerable period.

One interesting subdivision of this class consists of the Kâmarûpas of those anthropoid apes mentioned in *The Secret Doctrine* who are already individualized and will be ready to take human incarnation in the next round, or perhaps some of them even sooner. (Editor's note: See Vol. I, p. 184 of The Secret Doctrine (1888) by Blavatsky. This foundational work presents a cyclical view of the universe, emphasizing the interconnectedness of all things and the spiritual evolution of humanity. The text explores ideas of karma, reincarnation, and the unity of matter and energy, which resonate with both contemporary science and spirituality. Dense and symbolic, it requires readers to engage with abstract and esoteric ideas, offering a universal framework that bridges science, religion, and philosophy to understand existence.)

3. *Nature-Spirits of all Kinds.* So many and so varied are the subdivisions of this class that to do them anything like justice one would need to devote a separate treatise to this subject alone. Some characteristics, however, they all have in common, and it will be sufficient here to try to give some idea of those.

To begin with, we must realize that we are here dealing with entities which differ radically from all that we have hitherto considered. Though we may rightly classify the elemental essence and the animal Kâmarûpa as non-human, the monadic essence which manifests itself through them will, nevertheless, in the fulness of time, evolve to the level of manifesting itself through some future humanity comparable to our own, and if we were able to look back through countless ages on our own evolution in previous manvantaras, we should find that that which is now ourselves has passed on its upward path through similar stages.

That, however, is not the case with the vast kingdom of nature-spirits; they neither have been, nor ever will be, members of a humanity such as ours; their line of evolution is entirely different, and their only connection with us consists in our temporary occupancy of the same planet. Of course, since we are neighbors for the time being we owe unneighborly kindness to one another when we happen to meet, but our lines of development differ so widely that each can do but little for the other.

Many writers have included these spirits among the elementals, and indeed they are the elementals (or perhaps, to speak more accurately, the animals) of a higher evolution. Though much more highly developed than our elemental essence, they have yet certain characteristics in common with it; for example, they also are divided into seven great classes, inhabiting respectively the same seven states of matter already mentioned as permeated by the corresponding varieties of the essence. Thus, to take those which are most readily comprehensible to us, there are spirits of the earth, water, air, and fire (or ether)—definite intelligent astral entities residing and functioning in each of those media. It may be asked how it is possible for any kind of creature to inhabit the solid substance of a rock, or of the crust of the earth.

The answer is that since the nature-spirits are formed of astral matter, the substance of the rock is no hindrance to their motion or their vision, and furthermore physical matter in its solid state is their natural element—the only one to which they are accustomed and in which they feel at home. The same is of course true of those who live in water, air or ether.

In medieval literature, these earth-spirits are often called gnomes, while the water-spirits are spoken of as ûndinés, the air-spirits as sylphs, and the ether-spirits as salamanders. In popular language they are known by many names—fairies, pixies, elves, brownies, peris, djinns, trolls, satyrs, fauns, kobolds, imps, goblins, good people, etc.—some of these titles being applied only to one variety, and others indiscriminately to all.

Their forms are many and various, but most frequently human in shape and somewhat diminutive in size. Like almost all inhabitants of the astral plane, they can assume any appearance at will, but they undoubtedly have definite forms of their own, or perhaps we should rather say favorite forms, which they wear when they have no special object in taking any other. Of course, under ordinary conditions they are not visible to physical sight at all, but they have the power of making themselves so by materialization when they wish to be seen.

There are an immense number of subdivisions or races among them, and individuals of these subdivisions differ in intelligence and disposition precisely as human beings do. The great majority of them apparently prefer to avoid man altogether; his habits and emanations are distasteful to them, and the constant rush of astral currents set up by his restless, ill-regulated desires disturbs and annoys them.

On the other hand, instances are not wanting in which nature-spirits have as it were made friends with human beings and offered them such assistance as lay in their power, as in the well-known stories told of the Scotch brownies or of the fire-lighting fairies mentioned in spiritualistic literature. This helpful attitude, however, is comparatively rare, and in most cases when they come in contact with man, they either show indifference or dislike, or else take an impish delight in deceiving him and playing childish tricks upon him.

Many a story illustrative of this curious characteristic may be found among the village gossip of the peasantry in almost any lonely mountainous district, and anyone who has been in the habit of attending *séances* for physical phenomena will recollect instances of practical joking and silly though usually good-natured horseplay, which always indicate the presence of some of the lower orders of the nature-spirits. They are greatly assisted in their tricks by the wonderful power which they possess of casting a glamour over those who yield themselves to their influence, so that such victims for the time see and hear only what these fairies impress upon them, exactly as the mesmerized subject sees, hears, feels and believes whatever the magnetizer wishes. The nature-spirits, however, have not the mesmerizer's power of dominating the human will, except in the case of quite unusually weak-minded people, or of those who allow themselves to fall into such a condition of helpless terror that their will is temporarily in abeyance; they cannot go beyond deception of the senses, but of that art they are undoubted masters, and cases are not wanting in which they have cast their glamour over a considerable number of people at once. It is by invoking their aid in the exercise of this peculiar power that some of the most wonderful feats of the Indian jugglers are performed—the entire audience being in fact hallucinated and made to imagine that they see and hear a whole series of events which have not really taken place at all.

We might almost look upon the nature-spirits as a kind of astral humanity, but for the fact that none of them—not even the highest possess a permanent reincarnating individuality. Apparently therefore one point in which their line of evolution differs from ours is that a much greater proportion of intelligence is developed before permanent individualization takes place; but of the stages through which they have passed, and those through which they have yet to pass, we can know little. The life-periods of the different subdivisions vary greatly, some being quite short, others much longer than our human lifetime.

We stand so entirely outside such a life as theirs that it is impossible for us to understand much about its conditions; but it appears overall to be a simple, joyous, irresponsible kind of existence, much such as a party of happy children might lead among exceptionally favorable physical surroundings. Though tricky and mischievous, they are rarely malicious unless provoked by some unwarrantable intrusion or annoyance; but as a body they also partake to some extent of the universal feeling of distrust for man, and they generally seem inclined to resent somewhat the first appearance of a neophyte on the astral plane, so that he usually makes their acquaintance under some unpleasant or terrifying form.

If, however, he declines to be frightened by any of their freaks, they soon accept him as a necessary evil and take no further notice of him, while some among them may even after a time become friendly and manifest pleasure on meeting him.

Some among the many subdivisions of this class are much less childlike and more dignified than those we have been describing, and it is from these sections that the entities who have sometimes been reverenced under the name of wood-gods, or local village-gods, have been drawn. Such entities would be quite sensible of the flattery involved in the reverence shown to them, would enjoy it, and would no doubt be quite ready to do any small service they could in return. (The village-god is also often an artificial entity, but that variety will be considered in its appropriate place.)

The Adept knows how to make use of the services of the nature-spirits when he requires them, but the ordinary magician can obtain their assistance only by processes either of invocation or evocation—that is, either by attracting their attention as a suppliant and making some kind of bargain with them, or by endeavoring to set in motion influences which would compel their obedience.

Both methods are extremely undesirable, and the latter is also excessively dangerous, as the operator would arouse a determined hostility which might prove fatal to him. Needless to say, no one studying occultism under a qualified Master would ever be permitted to attempt anything of the kind at all.

4. *The Devas.* The highest system of evolution connected with this earth, so far as we know, is that of the beings whom Hindus call the Devas, and who have elsewhere been spoken of as angels, sons of God, etc.

They may, in fact, be regarded as a kingdom lying next above humanity, in the same way as humanity in turn lies next above the animal kingdom, but with this important difference, that while for an animal there is no possibility of evolution through any kingdom but the human, man, when he attains a certain high level, finds various paths of advancement opening before him, of which this great Deva evolution is only one. In comparison with the sublime renunciation of the Nirmânakâya, the acceptance of this line of evolution is sometimes spoken of in the books as "yielding to the temptation to become a god," but it must not be inferred from this expression that any shadow of blame attaches to the man who makes this choice.

The path he selects is not the shortest, but it is nevertheless a very noble one, and if his developed intuition impels him towards it, it is probably the one best suited for his capacities. We must never forget that in spiritual as in physical climbing it is not everyone who can bear the strain of the steeper path.

There may be many for whom what seems the slower way is the only one possible, and we should indeed be unworthy followers of the great Teachers if we allowed our ignorance to betray us into the slightest thought of despisal towards those whose choice differs from our own.

However confident that ignorance of the difficulties of the future may allow us to feel now, it is impossible for us to tell at this stage what we shall find ourselves able to do when, after many lives of patient striving, we have earned the right to choose our own future; and indeed, even those who "yield to the temptation to become gods," have a sufficiently glorious career before them, as will presently be seen. To avoid possible misunderstanding, it may be mentioned *par parenthèse* that there is another and entirely evil sense sometimes attached in books to this phrase of "becoming a god," but in that form it certainly could never be any kind of "temptation" to the developed man, and in any case, it is altogether foreign to our present subject. (Editor's note: *Par parenthèse* is a French phrase that translates to "by the way" or "in parentheses" in English. It is typically used to introduce a side comment, additional information, or something that is not central to the main topic but is worth mentioning.)

In oriental literature, this word "Deva" is frequently used vaguely to mean almost any kind of non-human entity, so that it would often include Dhyân Chohans on the one hand and nature-spirits and artificial elementals on the other.

Here, however, its use will be restricted to the magnificent evolution which we are now considering. Though connected with this earth, the Devas are by no means confined to it, for the whole of our present chain of seven worlds is as one world to them, their evolution being through a grand system of seven chains. Their hosts have hitherto been recruited chiefly from other humanities in the solar system, some lower and some higher than ours, since but a very small portion of our own has as yet reached the level at which for us it is possible to join them; but it seems certain that some of their very numerous classes have not passed in their upward progress through any humanity at all comparable to ours.

It is not possible for us at present to understand very much about them, but it is clear that what may be described as the aim of their evolution is considerably higher than ours; that is to say, while the object of our human evolution is to raise the successful portion of humanity to a certain degree of occult development by the end of the seventh round, the object of the Deva evolution is to raise their foremost rank to a very much higher level in the corresponding period. For them, as for us, a steeper but shorter path to still more sublime heights lies open to earnest endeavor; but what those heights may be in their case we can only conjecture.

It is of course only the lower fringe of this august body that need be mentioned in connection with our subject of the astral plane. Their three lower great divisions (beginning from the bottom) are generally called Kâmadevas, Rûpadevas, and Arûpadevas respectively. Just as our ordinary body here—the lowest body possible for us—is the physical, so the ordinary body of a Kâmadeva is the astral; so that he stands in somewhat the same position as humanity will do when it reaches planet F, and he, living ordinarily in an astral body, would go out of it to higher spheres in a Mâyâvirûpa just as we might in an astral body, while to enter the Kârana Sharîra would be to him (when sufficiently developed) no greater effort than to form a Mâyâvirûpa is to us.

In the same way the Rûpadeva's ordinary body would be the Mâyâvirûpa, since his habitat is on the four lower or rûpa levels of that spiritual state which we usually call Devachan: while the Arûpadeva belongs to the three higher levels of that plane and owns no nearer approach to a body than the Kârana Sharîra. But for Rûpa and Arûpadevas to manifest on the astral plane is an occurrence at least as rare as it is for astral entities to materialize on this physical plane, so we need do no more than mention them now.

As regards the lowest division—the Kâmadevas—it would be quite a mistake to think of all of them as immeasurably superior to ourselves, since some have entered their ranks from a humanity in some respects less advanced than our own; of course the general average among them is much higher than among us, for all that is actively or willfully evil has long been weeded out from their ranks; but they differ widely in disposition, and a really noble, unselfish, spiritually-minded man may well stand higher in the scale of evolution than some of them.

Their attention can be attracted by certain magical evocations, but the only kind of human agency that can dominate theirs is that of a certain high class of Adepts. As a rule, they seem scarcely conscious of us on our physical plane, but it does now and then happen that one of them becomes aware of some human difficulty which excites his pity, and he perhaps renders some assistance, just as any of us would try to help an animal that we saw in trouble. But it is well understood among them that any interference in human affairs at the present stage is likely to do far more harm than good. Above the Arûpadevas there are four other great divisions, and again, above and beyond the Deva kingdom altogether, stand the great hosts of the Dhyân Chohans, but the consideration of such glorified Beings would be out of place in an essay on the astral plane.

Though we cannot claim them as belonging exactly to any of our classes, this is perhaps the best place in which to mention those wonderful and important Beings, the four Devarâjahs. In this name the word Deva must not, however, be taken in the sense in which we have been using it, for it is not over the Deva kingdom but over the four "elements" of earth, water, air, and fire, with their indwelling nature-spirits and essences, that these four Kings rule.

What the evolution has been through which they rose to their present height of power and wisdom we cannot tell, save only that it has certainly not passed through anything corresponding to our own humanity.

They are often spoken of as the Regents of the Earth, or Angels of the four cardinal points, and the Hindu books call them the Chatur Mahârâjahs, giving their names as Dhritarāshtra, Virūdhaka, Virūpaksha, and Vaishrāvana. In the same books their hosts are called Gandharvas, Kumbhandas, Nâgas, and Yakshas respectively, the points of the compass appropriated to each being in corresponding order east, south, west, and north, and their symbolical colors white, blue, red, and gold.

They are mentioned in *The Secret Doctrine* as "winged globes and fiery wheels"; and in the Christian bible Ezekiel makes a very remarkable attempt at a description of them in which very similar words are used. References to them are to be found in the symbology of every religion, and they have always been held in the highest reverence as the protectors of mankind. It is they who are the agents of man's Karma during his life on earth, and they thus play an extremely important part in human destiny. The Lipika the great karmic deities of the Kosmos, weigh the deeds of each personality when the final separation of its principles takes place in Kâmaloka and give as it were the mold of an etheric double exactly suitable to its Karma for the man's next birth; but it is the Devarâjahs who, having command of the "elements" of which that etheric double must be composed, arrange their proportion so as to fulfil accurately the intention of the Lipika.

It is they also who constantly watch all through life to counterbalance the changes perpetually being introduced into man's condition by his own free will and that of those around him, so that no injustice may be done, and Karma may be accurately worked out, if not in one way, then in another.

A learned dissertation upon these marvelous beings will be found in *The Secret Doctrine*. They are able to take human material forms at will, and several cases are recorded when they have done so. All the higher nature-spirits and hosts of artificial elementals act as their agents in the stupendous work they carry out, yet all the threads are in their hands, and the whole responsibility rests upon them alone.

It is not often that these beings manifest upon the astral plane, but when they do, they are the most remarkable of its non-human inhabitants.

A student of occultism will not need to be told that as there are seven great classes both of nature-spirits and elemental essence there must really be seven and not four Devarâjahs but outside the circle of initiation little is known and less may be said of the higher three.

(Editor's note: See *The Secret Doctrine* (1888), Vol. I, pp. 122-126. Blavatsky's dense, highly esoteric text seeks to synthesize occult science and metaphysics. The book is divided into two volumes: Cosmogenesis (Vol. I) and Anthropogenesis (Vol. II). Volume I focuses on the origins of the universe, exploring cosmic laws, cycles, and the metaphysical principles behind creation. Volume II focuses on the origins and evolution of humanity from a theosophical and esoteric perspective. It is worthwhile to compare and contract her work with that of the Jesuit mystic Teilhard de Chardin, whose work on the noosphere was later taken up by Silicon Valley tech culture in the 1990's and beyond. See: McFarlane, Duncan. "The Noosphere Is Here." Kosmos Journal, 2019, www.kosmosjournal.org/kj_article/the-noosphere-is-here/.)

ARTIFICIAL.

This, the largest class of astral entities, is also much the most important to man. Being entirely his own creation, it is inter-related with him by the closest karmic bonds, and its action upon him is direct and incessant. It is an enormous inchoate mass of semi-intelligent entities, differing among themselves as human thoughts differ, and practically incapable of anything like classification or arrangement.

The only division which can be usefully made is that which distinguishes between the artificial elementals made by the majority of mankind unconsciously, and those made by magicians with definite intent; while we may relegate to a third class the very small number of artificially arranged entities which are not elementals at all.

1. *Elementals formed unconsciously.* It has already been explained that the elemental essence which surrounds us on every side is in all its numberless varieties singularly susceptible to the influence of human thought.

The action of the mere casual wandering thought upon it, causing it to burst into a cloud of rapidly moving, evanescent forms, has already been described; we have now to note how it is affected when the human mind formulates a definite, purposeful thought or wish. The effect produced is of the most striking nature. The thought seizes upon the plastic essence, and molds it instantly into a living being of appropriate form—a being which when once thus created is in no way under the control of its creator, but lives out a life of its own, the length of which is proportionate to the intensity of the thought or wish which called it into existence. It lasts, in fact, just as long as the thought-force holds it together.

Most people's thoughts are so fleeting and indecisive that the elementals created by them last only a few minutes or a few hours, but an often-repeated thought or an earnest wish will form an elemental whose existence may extend to many days. Since the ordinary man's thoughts refer very largely to himself, the elementals they form remain hovering about him, and constantly tend to provoke a repetition of the idea they represent, since such repetitions, instead of forming new elementals, would strengthen the old one, and give it a fresh lease of life.

A man, therefore, who frequently dwells upon one wish often forms for himself an astral attendant which, constantly fed by fresh thought, may haunt him for years, ever gaining more and more strength and influence over him; and it will easily be seen that if the desire be an evil one the effect upon his moral nature may be of the most disastrous character.

Still more pregnant of result for good or evil are a man's thoughts about other people, for in that case they hover not about the thinker, but about the object of the thought. A kindly thought about any person or an earnest wish for his good will form and project towards him a friendly artificial elemental; if the wish be a definite one, as, for example, that he may recover from some sickness, then the elemental will be a force ever hovering over him to promote his recovery, or to ward off any influence that might tend to hinder it, and in doing this it will display what appears like a very considerable amount of intelligence and adaptability, though really it is simply a force acting along the line of least resistance—pressing steadily in one direction all the time, and taking advantage of any channel that it can find, just as the water in a cistern would in a moment find the one open pipe among a dozen closed ones, and proceed to empty itself through that.

If the wish be merely an indefinite one for his general good, the elemental essence in its wonderful plasticity will respond exactly to that less distinct idea also, and the creature formed will expend its force in the direction of whatever action for the man's advantage comes most readily to hand. Of course in all cases the amount of such force it has to expend, and the length of time that it will live to expend it, depend entirely upon the strength of the original wish or thought which gave it birth; though it must be remembered that it can be, as it were, fed and strengthened, and its life-period protracted by other good wishes or friendly thoughts projected in the same direction.

Furthermore, it appears to be actuated, like most other beings, by an instinctive desire to prolong its life, and thus reacts on its creator as a force constantly tending to provoke the renewal of the feeling which called it into existence. It also influences in a similar manner others with whom it comes into contact, though its *rapport* with them is naturally not so perfect.

All that has been said as to the effect of good wishes and friendly thoughts is also true in the opposite direction of evil wishes and angry thoughts; and considering the amount of envy, hatred, malice and all uncharitableness that exists in the world, it will be readily understood that among the artificial elementals many terrible creatures are to be seen.

A man whose thoughts or desires are spiteful, brutal, sensual, avaricious, moves through the world carrying with him everywhere a pestiferous atmosphere of his own, peopled with the loathsome beings he has created to be his companions, and thus is not only in sadly evil case himself, but is a dangerous nuisance to his fellow-men, subjecting all who have the misfortune to come into contact with him to the risk of moral contagion from the influence of the abominations with which he chooses to surround himself.

A feeling of envious or jealous hatred towards another person will send an evil elemental to hover over him and seek for a weak point through which it can operate; and if the feeling be a persistent one, such a creature may be continually nourished by it and thereby enabled to protract its undesirable activity for a very long period. It can, however, produce no effect upon the person towards whom it is directed unless he has himself some tendency which it can foster—some fulcrum for its lever, as it were; from the aura of a man of pure thought and good life all such influences at once rebound, finding nothing upon which they can fasten, and in that case, by a very curious law, they react in all their force upon their original creator. In him by the hypothesis they find a very congenial sphere of action, and thus the Karma of his evil wish works itself out at once by means of the very entity which he himself has called into existence.

It occasionally happens, however, that an artificial elemental of this description is for various reasons unable to expend its force either upon its object or its creator, and in such cases it becomes a kind of wandering demon, readily attracted by any person who indulges feelings similar to that which gave it birth, and equally prepared either to stimulate such feelings in him for the sake of the strength it may gain from them, or to pour out its store of evil influence upon him through any opening which he may offer it. If it is sufficiently powerful to seize upon and inhabit some passing shell it frequently does so, as the possession of such a temporary home enables it to husband its dreadful resources more carefully. In this form it may manifest through a medium, and by masquerading as some well-known friend may sometimes obtain an influence over people upon whom it would otherwise have little hold.

What has been written above will serve to enforce the statement already made as to the importance of maintaining a strict control over our thoughts. Many a well-meaning man, who is scrupulously careful to do his duty towards his neighbor in word and deed, is apt to consider that his thoughts at least are nobody's business but his own, and so lets them run riot in various directions, utterly unconscious of the swarms of baleful creatures he is launching upon the world.

To such a man an accurate comprehension of the effect of thought and desire in producing artificial elementals would come as a horrifying revelation; on the other hand, it would be the greatest consolation to many devoted and grateful souls who are oppressed with the feeling that they are unable to do anything in return for the kindness lavished upon them by their benefactors. For friendly thoughts and earnest good wishes are as easily and as effectually formulated by the poorest as by the richest, and it is within the power of almost any man, if he will take the trouble, to maintain what is practically a good angel always at the side of the brother or sister, the friend or the child whom he loves best, no matter in what part of the world he may be.

Many a time a mother's loving thoughts and prayers have formed themselves into an angel guardian for the child, and except in the almost impossible case that the child had in him no instinct responsive to a good influence, have undoubtedly given him assistance and protection.

Such guardians may often be seen by clairvoyant vision, and there have even been cases where one of them has had sufficient strength to materialize and become for the moment visible to physical sight. A curious fact which deserves mention here is that even after the passage of the mother into the devachanic condition the love which she pours out upon the children she thinks of as surrounding her will react upon the real children still living in this world and will often support the guardian elemental which she created while on earth, until her dear ones themselves pass away in turn.

As Madame Blavatsky remarks, "her love will always be felt by the children in the flesh; it will manifest in their dreams and often in various events, in providential protections and escapes—for love is a strong shield and is not limited by space or time."[1] All the stories of the intervention of guardian angels must not, however, be attributed to the action of artificial elementals, for in many cases such "angels" have been the souls of either living or recently departed human beings, and they have also occasionally, though rarely, been Devas.

This power of an earnest desire, especially if frequently repeated, to create an active elemental which ever presses forcefully in the direction of its own fulfilment, is the scientific explanation of what devout but unphilosophical people describe as answers to prayer. There are occasions, though at present these are rare, when the Karma of the person so praying is such as to permit of assistance being directly rendered to him by an Adept or his pupil, and there is also the still rarer possibility of the intervention of a Deva or some friendly nature-spirit; but in these cases the easiest and most obvious form for such assistance to take would be the strengthening and the intelligent direction of the elemental already formed by the wish.

A very curious and instructive instance of the extreme persistence of these artificial elementals under favorable circumstances came under the notice of one of our investigators quite recently.

All readers of the literature of such subjects are aware that many of our ancient families are supposed to have associated with them a traditional death-warning—a phenomenon of one kind or another which foretells, usually some days beforehand, the approaching decease of the head of the house. A picturesque example of this is the well-known story of the white bird of the Oxenhams, whose appearance has ever since the time of Queen Elizabeth been recognized as a sure presage of the death of some member of the family; while another is the spectral coach which is reported to drive up to the door of a certain castle in the north when a similar calamity is impending.

A phenomenon of this order occurs in connection with the family of one of our members, but it is of a much commoner and less striking type than either of the above, consisting only of a solemn and impressive strain of dirge-like music, which is heard apparently floating in the air three days before the death takes place. Our member, having himself twice heard this mystic sound, finding its warning in both cases quite accurate, and knowing also that according to family tradition the same thing had been happening for several centuries, set himself to seek by occult methods for the cause underlying so strange a phenomenon. The result was rather unexpected but interesting.

It appeared that somewhere in the twelfth century the head of the family went to the crusades, like many another valiant man, and took with him to win his spurs in the sacred cause his youngest and favorite son, a promising youth whose success in life was the dearest wish of his father's heart. Unhappily, however, the young man was killed in battle, and the father was plunged into the depths of despair, lamenting not only the loss of his son, but still more the fact that he was cut off so suddenly in the full flush of careless and not altogether blameless youth.

So poignant, indeed, were the old man's feelings that he cast off his knightly armor and joined one of the great monastic orders, vowing to devote all the remainder of his life to prayer, first for the soul of his son, and secondly that henceforward no descendant of his might ever again encounter what seemed to his simple and pious mind the terrible danger of meeting death unprepared. Day after day for many a year he poured all the energy of his soul into the channel of that one intense wish, firmly believing that somehow or other the result he so earnestly desired would be brought about.

A student of occultism will have little difficulty in deciding what would be the effect of such a definite and long-continued stream of thought; our knightly monk created an artificial elemental of immense power and resourcefulness for its own object, and accumulated within it a store of force which would enable it to carry out his wishes for an indefinite period.

An elemental is a perfect storage-battery—one from which there is practically no leakage; and when we remember what its original strength must have been, and how comparatively rarely it would be called upon to put it forth, we shall scarcely wonder that even now it exhibits unimpaired vitality, and still warns the direct descendants of the old crusader of their approaching doom by repeating in their ears the strange wailing music which was the dirge of a young and valiant soldier seven hundred years ago in Palestine.

2. *Elementals formed consciously.* Since such results as have been described above have been achieved by the thought-force of men who were entirely in the dark as to what they were doing, it will readily be imagined that a magician who understands the subject, and can see exactly what effect he is producing, may wield immense power along these lines.

As a matter of fact occultists of both the white and dark schools frequently use artificial elementals in their work, and few tasks are beyond the powers of such creatures when scientifically prepared and directed with knowledge and skill; for one who knows how to do so can maintain a connection with his elemental and guide it, no matter at what distance it may be working, so that it will practically act as though endowed with the full intelligence of its master.

Very definite and very efficient guardian angels have sometimes been supplied in this way, though it is probably very rarely that Karma permits such a decided interference in a person's life as that would be.

In such a case, however, as that of a pupil of the Adepts, who might have in the course of his work for them to run the risk of attack from forces with which his unaided strength would be entirely insufficient to cope, guardians of this description have been given, and have fully proved their sleepless vigilance and their tremendous power. By some of the more advanced processes of black magic, also, artificial elementals of immense power may be called into existence. Much evil has been worked in various ways by such entities.

But it is true of them, as of the previous class, that if they are aimed at a person whom by reason of his purity of character they are unable to influence they react with terrible force upon their creator; so that the medieval story of the magician being torn to pieces by the fiends he himself had raised is no mere fable, but may well have an awful foundation in fact.

Such creatures occasionally, for various reasons, escape from the control of those who are trying to make use of them, and become wandering and aimless demons, as do some of those mentioned under the previous heading under similar circumstances; but those that we are considering, having much more intelligence and power, and a much longer existence, are proportionately more dangerous. They invariably seek for means of prolonging their life either by feeding like vampires upon the vitality of human beings, or by influencing them to make offerings to them; and among simple half-savage tribes they have frequently succeeded by judicious management in getting themselves recognized as village or family gods.

Any deity which demands sacrifices involving the shedding of blood may always be set down as belonging to the lowest and most loathsome class of this order; other less objectionable types are sometimes content with offerings of rice and cooked food of various kinds. There are parts of India where both these varieties may be found flourishing even at the present day, and in Africa they are probably comparatively numerous. By means of whatever nourishment they can obtain from the offerings, and still more by the vitality they draw from their devotees, they may continue to prolong their existence for many years, or even centuries, retaining sufficient strength to perform occasional phenomena of a mild type in order to stimulate the faith and zeal of their followers, and invariably making themselves unpleasant in some way or other if the accustomed sacrifices are neglected.

For example, it was asserted recently that in one Indian village the inhabitants had found that whenever for any reason the local deity did not get his or her regular meals, spontaneous fires began to break out with alarming frequency among the cottages, sometimes three or four simultaneously, in cases where they declared it was impossible to suspect human agency; and other stories of a more or less similar nature will no doubt recur to the memory of any reader who knows something of the out-of-the-way corners of that most wonderful of all countries.

The art of manufacturing artificial elementals of extreme virulence and power seems to have been one of the specialties of the magicians of Atlantis—"the lords of the dark face". One example of their capabilities in this line is given in *The Secret Doctrine* where we read of the wonderful speaking animals who had to be quieted by an offering of blood, lest they should awaken their masters and warn them of the impending destruction.[2]

But apart from these strange beasts they created other artificial entities of power and energy so tremendous, that it is darkly hinted that some of them have kept themselves in existence even to this day, though it is more than eleven thousand years since the cataclysm which overwhelmed their original masters. The terrible Indian goddess whose devotees were impelled to commit in her name the awful crimes of Thuggee—the ghastly Kâlí, worshipped even to this day with rites too abominable to be described—might well be a relic of a system which had to be swept away even at the cost of the submergence of a continent, and the loss of sixty-five million human lives.

3. *Human Artificials.* We have now to consider a class of entities which, though it contains but very few individuals, has acquired from its intimate connection with one of the great movements of modern times an importance entirely out of proportion to its numbers. It seems doubtful whether it should appear under the first or third of our main divisions; but, though certainly human, it is so far removed

from the course of ordinary evolution, so entirely the product of a will outside of its own, that it perhaps falls most naturally into place among the artificial beings.

The easiest way of describing it will be to commence with its history, and to do that we must once more look back to the great Atlantean race. In thinking of the Adepts and schools of occultism of that remarkable people our minds instinctively revert to the evil practices of which we hear so much in connection with their latter days; but we must not forget that before that age of selfishness and degradation the mighty civilization of Atlantis had brought forth much that was noble and worthy of admiration, and that among its leaders were some who now stand upon the loftiest pinnacles as yet attained by man.

Among the lodges for occult study preliminary to initiation formed by the Adepts of the good Law was one in a certain part of America which was then tributary to one of the great Atlantean monarchs—"the Divine Rulers of the Golden Gate"; and though it has passed through many and strange vicissitudes, though it has had to move its headquarters from country to country as each in turn was invaded by the jarring elements of a later civilization, that lodge still exists even at the present day, observing still the same old-world ritual even teaching as a sacred and hidden language the same Atlantean tongue which was used at its foundation so many thousands of years ago.

It remains what it was from the first—a lodge of occultists of pure and philanthropic aims, which can lead those students whom it finds worthy no inconsiderable distance on the road to knowledge and confers such psychic powers as are in its gift only after the most searching tests as to the fitness of the candidate. Its teachers do not stand upon the Adept level, yet hundreds have learnt through it how to set their feet upon the Path which has led them to Adeptship in later lives; and though it is not in direct communication with the Brotherhood of the Himalayas, there are some among the latter who have themselves been connected with it in former incarnations, and therefore retain a more than ordinarily friendly interest in its proceedings.

The chiefs of this lodge, though they have always kept themselves and their society strictly in the background, have nevertheless done what they could from time to time to assist the progress of truth in the world, and some half-century ago, in despair at the rampant material- ism which seemed to be stifling all spirituality in Europe and Amer- ica, they determined to make an attempt to combat it by somewhat novel methods—in point of fact to offer opportunities by which any reasonable man could acquire absolute proof of that life apart from the physical body which it was the tendency of science to deny.

The phenomena exhibited were not in themselves absolutely new, since in some form or other we may hear of them all through history; but their definite organization—their production as it were to or- der—these were features distinctly new to the modern world.

The movement they thus set on foot gradually grew into the vast fabric of modern spiritualism, and though it would perhaps be unfair to hold the originators of the scheme directly responsible for many of the results which have followed, we must admit that they have achieved their purpose to the extent of converting vast numbers of people from a belief in nothing in particular to a firm faith in at any rate some kind of future life.

This is undoubtedly a magnificent result, though, in the opinion of many of those whose power and knowledge enable them to take a wider view of such matters than we can, it has been attained at too great a cost, since it seems to them that on the whole the harm done outweighs the good. The method adopted was to take some ordinary person after death, arouse him thoroughly upon the astral plane, in- struct him to a certain extent in the powers and possibilities belong- ing to it, and then put him in charge of a spiritualistic circle.

He in his turn "developed" other departed personalities along the same line, they all acted upon those who sat at their *séances*, and "de- veloped" them as mediums; and so spiritualism grew and flourished.

No doubt living members of the original lodge occasionally manifested themselves in astral form at some of the circles—perhaps they may do so even now; but in most cases they simply gave such direction and guidance as they considered necessary to the persons they had put in charge. There is little doubt that the movement increased so much more rapidly than they had expected that it soon got quite beyond their control, so that, as has been said, for many of the later developments they can only be held indirectly responsible.

Of course the intensification of the astral-plane life in those persons who were thus put in charge of circles distinctly delayed their natural progress; and though the idea had been that anything lost in this way would be fully atoned for by the good Karma gained by helping to lead others to the truth, it was soon found that it was impossible to make use of a "spirit-guide" for any length of time without doing him serious and permanent injury.

In some cases, such "guides" were therefore withdrawn, and others substituted for them; in others it was considered for various reasons undesirable to make such a change, and then a very remarkable expedient was adopted which gave rise to the curious class of creatures we have called "human artificials."

The higher principles of the original "guide" were allowed to pass on their long-delayed evolution into the devachanic condition, but the shade he left behind him was taken possession of, sustained, and operated upon so that it might appear to its admiring circle practically just as before.

This seems at first to have been done by members of the lodge themselves, but apparently that arrangement was found irksome or unsuitable, or perhaps was considered a waste of force, and the same objection applied to the use for this purpose of an artificial elemental; so it was eventually decided that the departed person who would have been appointed to succeed the late "spirit-guide" should still do so, but should take possession of the latter's shade or shell, and in fact simply wear his appearance.

It is said that some members of the lodge objected to this on the ground that though the purpose might be entirely good a certain amount of deception was involved; but the general opinion seems to have been that as the shade really was the same, and contained something at any rate of the original lower Manas, there was nothing that could be called deception in the matter.

This, then, was the genesis of the human artificial entity, and it is understood that in some cases more than one such change has been made without arousing suspicion, though on the other hand some investigators of spiritualism have remarked on the fact that after a considerable lapse of time certain differences suddenly became observable in the manner and disposition of a "spirit."

It is needless to say that none of the Adept Brotherhood has ever approved of the formation of an artificial entity of this sort, though they could not interfere with anyone who thought it right to take such a course.

A weak point in the arrangement is that many others besides the original lodge may adopt this plan, and there is nothing whatever to prevent black magicians from supplying communicating "spirits"—as, indeed, they have been known to do.

With this class we conclude our survey of the inhabitants of the astral plane. With the reservations specially made some few pages back, the catalogue may be taken as a fairly complete one; but it must once more be emphasized that this treatise claims only to sketch the merest outline of a very vast subject, the detailed elaboration of which would need a lifetime of study and hard work.

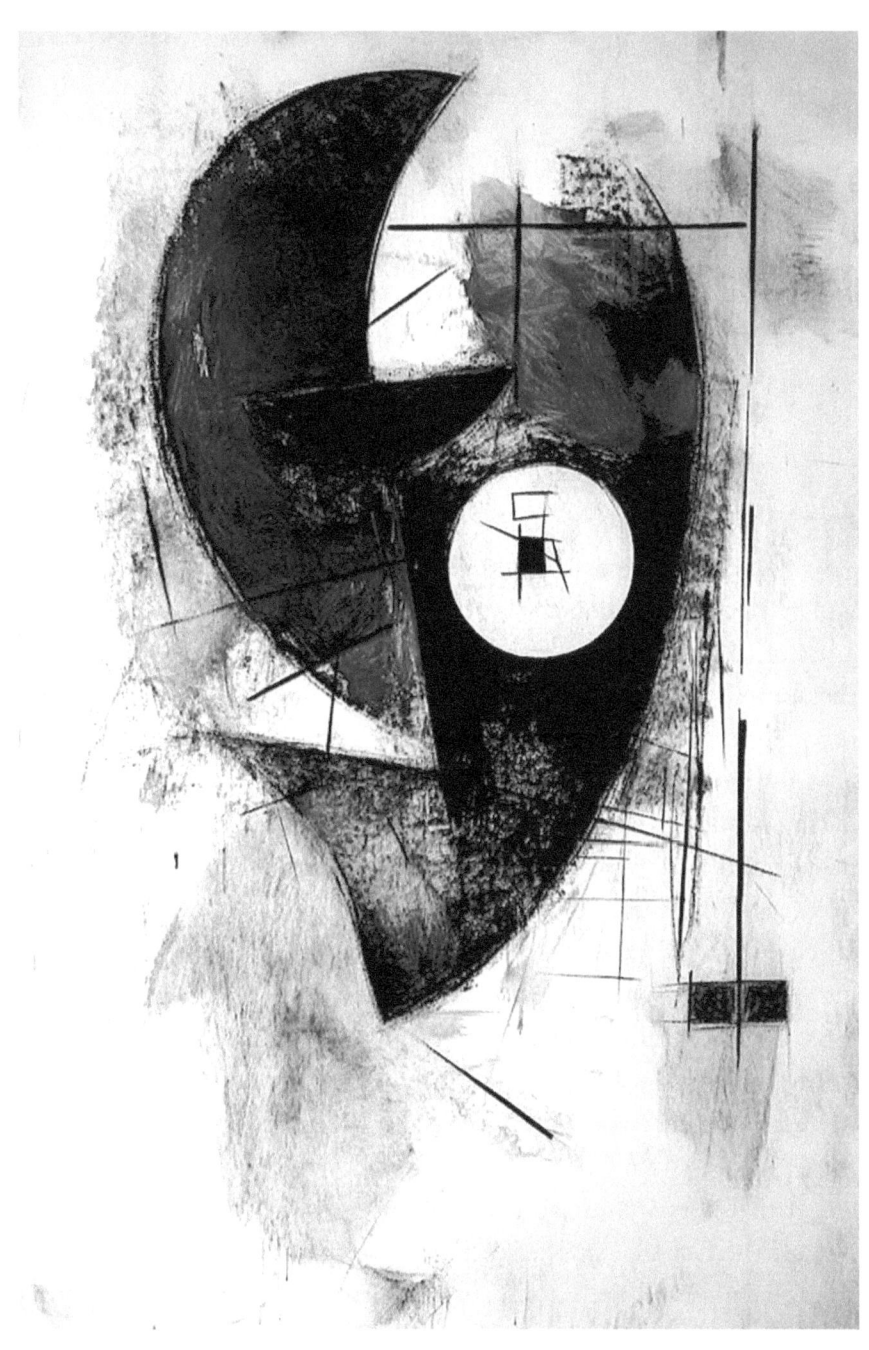

5

※

PHENOMENA.

Though in the course of this little book various superphysical phenomena have been mentioned and to some extent explained, it will perhaps, before concluding, be desirable to recapitulate as to give a list of those which are most frequently met with by the student of these subjects, and to show by which of the agencies we have attempted to describe they are usually caused.

The resources of the astral world, however, are so varied that almost any phenomenon with which we are acquainted can be produced in several different ways, so that it is only possible to lay down rules in a general manner.

Apparitions or ghosts furnish a very good instance of the remark just made, for in the loose way in which the words are ordinarily used, they may stand for almost any inhabitant of the astral plane. Of course, psychically developed people are constantly seeing such things, but for an ordinary person to "see a ghost," as the common expression runs, one of two things must happen. Either that ghost must materialize, or that person must have a temporary flash of psychic perception. But for the fact that neither of these events is a common one, ghosts would be met with in our streets as frequently if not more frequently than living people.

Churchyard and Ghost: If the ghost is seen hovering about a grave it is probably the etheric shell of a newly-buried person, though it *may* be the astral body of a living man haunting in sleep the tomb of a friend.

Or again, it may be a materialized thought-form—that is, an artificial elemental created by the energy with which a man thinks of himself as present at that particular spot. These varieties would be easily distinguishable one from the other by any one accustomed to use astral vision, but an unpracticed person would be quite likely to call them all vaguely "ghosts."

Apparitions of the dying: Apparitions at the time of death are by no means uncommon. They are very often appearances by the astral form of the dying man just before what we elect to call the moment of dissolution. Though here again, they are quite likely to be thought-forms called into being by his earnest wish to see some friend once more before he passes into an unfamiliar condition.

Haunted Locations: Apparitions at the spot where some crime was committed are usually thought-forms projected by the criminal, who, whether living or dead, but most especially when dead, is perpetually thinking over again and again the circumstances of his action.

And since these thoughts are especially vivid in his mind near the anniversary of the original crime, it is often on that occasion that the artificial elementals he creates are strong enough to materialize themselves to ordinary sight—a fact which accounts for the periodicity of some manifestations of this class.

Another point in reference to such phenomena is, that wherever any tremendous mental disturbance has taken place, wherever overwhelming terror, pain, sorrow, hatred, or indeed any kind of intense passion has been felt, an impression of so very marked a character has been made upon the astral light that a person with even the faintest glimmer of psychic faculty cannot but be deeply impressed by it, and it would need but a slight temporary increase of sensibility to enable him to visualize the entire scene—to see the event in all its detail apparently taking place before his very eyes—and in such a case he would of course report that the place was haunted, and that he had seen a ghost.

Indeed, people who are as yet unable to see psychically under any circumstances are frequently very unpleasantly impressed when visiting such places as we have mentioned.

There are many, for example, who feel uncomfortable when passing the site of Tyburn Tree. (Editor's note: The Tyburn Tree was one an infamous site of public execution in England. Used from the 12th century until 1783, it gained notoriety as a symbol of retribution. The gallows, installed in 1571, was a triangular structure made of three uprights and a horizontal crossbeam, allowing for multiple executions at once—up to 24 individuals could theoretically be hanged simultaneously. Gulp! Those sentenced to die at Tyburn (thieves, murderers, and political or religious figures such as Catholic martyr Edmund Campion), were paraded through the streets from Newgate Prison along what was known as "Tyburn Way."

Today, the site of the Tyburn Tree is marked by a plaque near Marble Arch. It has become an inadvertent tourist attraction for those interested in "trauma tourism;" visitors seek places linked to suffering or death. More interestingly, the Tyburn Tree is an example of the pre-modern justice system that Michel Foucault critiques in his seminal work, *Discipline and Punish: The Birth of the Prison* (1975). Foucault argues that punishment in the pre-modern era focused on public spectacle and physical retribution. Sites like Tyburn were designed not merely to punish criminals but to dramatize the sovereign's power through the public display of justice. The crowd's participation—whether through jeering, cheering, or silent observation—ensured that executions reinforced societal norms and demonstrated the consequences of defying authority.

Foucault contrasts this earlier model with the transformation that occurred in the late 18th and early 19th centuries, when punishment shifted away from public displays toward the modern disciplinary system, focused on surveillance, correction, and the internalization of control. The body, once the primary site of punishment, became secondary to the reform of the mind. Institutions like prisons and schools emerged as instruments of this new form of discipline, where individuals were monitored and normalized rather than punished publicly.)

Like those passing Tyburn with unease, others or cannot stay in the Chamber of Horrors at Madame Tussaud's, though they may not be in the least aware that their discomfort is due to the dreadful impressions in the astral light which surround places and objects redolent of horror and crime, and to the presence of the loathsome astral entities which always swarm about such centers.

(Editor's note: Madame Tussauds, founded by Marie Tussaud in 1835, began as a space that showcased lifelike wax figures of infamous criminals and historical figures, like Dr. Crippen and Jack the Ripper, displayed in the notorious Chamber of Horrors. These figures captured the dark side of human nature, drawing in visitors with a blend of morbid curiosity and historical reflection. But, over time, the museum underwent a transformation, aligning with the rise of celebrity/consumer capitalism.

Today, Madame Tussauds is a sprawling, global franchise that reflects modern pop culture; the museum is now populated with figures like Kylie Jenner, a reality TV star and influencer known more for her self-marketing than any substantive contribution, Kim Kardashian, whose fame has been built on social media and scandals, and Justin Bieber, whose celebrity is often more about his controversies than his music. We see that Madame Tussauds has become less a site of cultural reflection and more a spectacle designed to cater to a consumer base hungry for easily digestible celebrity-tenders.)

Family Ghosts: The family ghost, whom we generally find in the stock stories of the supernatural as an appanage of the feudal castle, may be either a thought-form or an unusually vivid impression in the astral light, or again he may really be an earth-bound ancestor still haunting the scenes in which his thoughts and hopes centered during life.

Bell Ringing, Etc.: Another class of hauntings which take the form of bell-ringing, stone-throwing, door-knocking, or the breaking of crockery, has already been referred to, and is almost invariably the work of elemental forces, either set blindly in motion by the clumsy efforts of an ignorant person trying to attract the attention of his surviving friends, or intentionally employed by some childishly mischievous nature-spirit.

Fairies: The nature-spirits are also responsible for whatever of truth there may be in all the strange fairy stories which are so common in certain parts of the country. Sometimes a temporary accession of clairvoyance, which is by no means uncommon among the inhabitants of lonely mountainous regions, enables some belated wayfarer to watch their joyous gambols.

Sometimes strange tricks are played upon some terrified victim, and a glamour is cast over him, making him, for example, see houses and people where he knows none really exist.

And this is frequently no mere momentary delusion, for a man will sometimes go through quite a long series of imaginary but most striking adventures, and then suddenly find that all his brilliant surroundings have vanished in a moment, leaving him standing in some lonely valley or on some wind-swept plain.

On the other hand, it is by no means safe to accept as founded on fact all the popular legends on the subject, for the grossest superstition is often mingled with the theories of the peasantry about these beings, as was shown by a recent terrible murder case in Ireland.

To the same entities must be attributed a large portion of what are called physical phenomena at spiritualistic *séances*—indeed, many a *séance* has been given entirely by these mischievous creatures.

And such a performance might easily include many very striking items, such as the answering of questions and delivery of pretended messages by raps or tilts, the exhibition of "spirit lights," the apport of objects from a distance, the reading of thoughts which were in the mind of any person present, the precipitation of writings or drawings, and even materializations.

In fact, the nature-spirits alone, if any of them happened to be disposed to take the trouble, could give a *séance* equal to the most wonderful of which we read.

For though there may be certain phenomena which they would not find it easy to reproduce, their marvelous power of glamour would enable them without difficulty to persuade the entire circle that these phenomena also had duly occurred, unless, indeed, there were present a trained observer who understood their arts and knew how to defeat them.

(Editor's note: *Glamour* originally comes from the Scottish *gramarye*, which referred to magic or enchantment, and was derived from the Old French *gramaire* (meaning grammar or learning). The word *gramaire* itself came from the Latin *grammatica* (meaning grammar or knowledge), which in medieval times was associated with occult or arcane knowledge. Over time, *gramarye* evolved to signify an alluring or deceptive spell, and by the early 18th century, the word *glamour* began to be used in English to refer to a spell, particularly one that produced an illusion of beauty. By the 19th century, the semantic cloud of the word had broadened to refer to a deceptive attractiveness or allure, especially in contexts like fashion or cinema. Today, in American society, glamour connotes physical attractiveness, frequently associated with celebrity culture, fashion, and media portrayals of beauty.)

Generally, whenever silly tricks or practical jokes are played at a *séance*, we may infer the presence either of low-class nature-spirits, or of human beings who were of a sufficiently degraded type to find pleasure in such idiotic performances during life.

Communicating Entities: As to the entities who may "communicate" at a *séance*, or may obsess and speak through an entranced medium, their name is simply legion; there is hardly a single class among all the varied inhabitants of the astral plane from whose ranks they may not be drawn, though after the explanations given it will be readily understood that the chances are very much against their coming from a high one.

A manifesting "spirit" *may* be exactly what it professes to be, but on the whole the probabilities are that it is nothing of the kind; and for the ordinary sitter there is absolutely no means of distinguishing the true from the false, since the extent to which a being having all the resources of the astral plane at his command can delude a person on the physical plane is so great that no reliance can be placed even on what seems the most convincing proof.

If something manifests which announces itself as a man's long-lost brother, he can have no certainty that its claim is a just one.

If it tells him of some fact known only to that brother and to himself, he remains unconvinced, for he knows that it might easily have read the information from his own mind, or from his surroundings in the astral light; even if it goes still further and tells him something connected with his brother, of which he himself is unaware, but which he afterwards verifies, he still realizes that even this may have been read from the astral record, or that what he sees before him may be only the shade of his brother, and so possess his memory without in any way being himself.

It is not for one moment denied that important communications have sometimes been made at *séances* by entities who in such cases have been precisely what they said they were; all that is claimed is that it is quite impossible for the ordinary person who visits a *séance* ever to be certain that he is not being cruelly deceived in one or other of half a dozen different ways. (Editor's note: The term *séance* comes from the French *séance* ("session" or "sitting"), derived from *séoir* ("to sit"). It was associated with spiritual communication in the 19th century, particularly with the Fox Sisters in 1848, who contacted a murdered peddler through rapping sounds, sparking the rise of the Spiritualist movement.

Key figures like Eusapia Palladino, Allan Kardec, and Arthur Conan Doyle supported the practice, with Kardec codifying Spiritualism in *The Spirits' Book* (1857) and Doyle defending *séances* after his son's death. Though *séances* were often debunked by figures like Harry Houdini, critiques of Western skepticism emerged, particularly from philosophers like Ralph Waldo Emerson and William James, who challenged the limitations of empirical science in texts such as *The Over-Soul* and *The Varieties of Religious Experience*.)

There have been a few cases in which members of the lodge of occultists referred to above as originating the spiritualistic movement have themselves given, through a medium, a series of valuable teachings on deeply interesting subjects, but this has invariably been at strictly private family *séances*, not at public performances for which money has been paid.

Astral Resources: To understand the methods by which a large class of physical phenomena are produced, it is necessary to have some comprehension of the various resources mentioned above, which a person functioning on the astral plane finds at his command. This is a branch of the subject which it is by no means easy to make clear, especially as it is hedged about with certain obviously necessary restrictions. It may perhaps help us if we remember that the astral plane may be regarded as in many ways only an extension of the physical, and the idea that matter may assume the etheric state (in which, though intangible to us, it is yet purely physical) may show us how the one melts into the other.

In fact, in the Hindu conception of Jagrat, or "the waking state," the physical and astral planes are combined, its seven subdivisions corresponding to the four conditions of physical matter, and the three broad divisions of astral matter explained above. With this thought in mind, it is easy to move a step further, and grasp the idea that astral vision, or rather astral perception, may from one point of view be defined as the capability of receiving an enormously increased number of different sets of vibrations.

The mind extends during projection in a way both stochastic and structured, adapting to unknown variables while maintaining an internal logic. Upon returning, it does not reconfigure itself exactly as it was, often altered by the journey in ways that influence perception, memory, and thought.

In our physical bodies one small set of slow vibrations is perceptible to us as sound; another small set of much more rapid vibrations affects us as light; and again, another set as electric action: but there are immense numbers of intermediate vibrations which produce no result which our physical senses can interpret at all.

Now it will readily be seen that if all, or even some only, of these intermediates, with all the complications producible by differences of wavelength, are perceptible on the astral plane, our comprehension of nature might be very greatly increased on that level, and we might be able to acquire much information which is now hidden from us.

Clairvoyance: It is admitted that some of these entities pass through solid matter with perfect ease, so that this enables us to account scientifically for some of the peculiarities of astral vision, though those minds to which the theory of the fourth dimension commends itself find in it a neater and more complete explanation.

It is clear that the mere possession of astral vision by a being would at once account for his capability to produce many results that seem very wonderful to us—such, for example, as the reading of a passage from a closed book; and when we remember, furthermore, that this faculty includes the power of thought-reading to the fullest extent, and also, when combined with the knowledge of the projection of currents in the astral light, that of observing a desired object in almost any part of the world, we see that a good many of the phenomena of clairvoyance are explicable even without rising above this level.

Of course, true, trained, and absolutely reliable clairvoyance calls into operation an entirely different set of faculties, but as these belong to a higher plane than the astral, they form no part of our present subject.

The faculty of accurate prevision, again, appertains altogether to that higher plane, yet flashes or reflections of it can show themselves to purely astral sight, more especially among simple-minded people—what is called "second-sight" among the Highlanders of Scotland being a well-known example.

Second Sight: Another fact which must not be forgotten is that any intelligent inhabitant of the astral plane is not only able to perceive these etheric vibrations but can also—if he has learned how it is done—adapt them to his own ends or himself set them in motion. (Editor's note: *second-sight,* the ability to perceive future events or communicate with spirits, was a notable belief among the Highlanders of Scotland, particularly in the 17th and 18th centuries. One famous case is that of Angus McDonald, a Highlander who reportedly predicted his own death in battle. Second-sight shows up in Scottish literature, such as in James Macpherson's *Ossian* poems and in Sir Walter Scott's novel *The Highland Widow* (1830). It also appears in art and films, including the 2008 film *Second Sight*, which draws on Scottish folklore, and various works by Scottish painter John Duncan.)

Astral Forces: It will be readily understood that superphysical forces and the methods of managing them are not subjects about which much can be written for publication at present, though there is reason to suppose that it may not be very long before at any rate some applications of one or two of them come to be known to the world at large.

It may perhaps be possible, without transgressing the limits of the permissible, to give so much of an idea of them as shall be sufficient to show in outline how certain phenomena are performed.

All who have much experience of spiritualistic *séances* at which physical results are produced must at one time or another have seen evidence of the employment of practically resistless force in, for example, the instantaneous movement of enormous weights, and so on.

And if of a scientific turn of mind, they may perhaps have wondered whence this force was obtained, and what was leverage employed.

Etheric Currents Pressure and Latent Energy: As usual in connection with astral phenomena, there are several ways in which such work may have been done, but it will be enough for the moment to hint at four.

First, there are great etheric currents constantly sweeping over the surface of the earth from pole to pole in volume which makes their power as irresistible as that of the rising tide, and there are methods by which this stupendous force may be safely utilized, though unskillful attempts to control it would be fraught with frightful danger.

Secondly, there is what can best be described as an etheric pressure, somewhat corresponding to, though immensely greater than, the atmospheric pressure. In ordinary life we are as little conscious of one of these pressures as we are of the other, but nevertheless they both exist, and if science were able to exhaust the ether from a given space, as it can exhaust the air, the one could be proved as readily as the other.

The difficulty of doing that lies in the fact that matter in the etheric condition freely inter-penetrates matter in all states below it, so that there is as yet no means within the knowledge of our physicists by which any given body of ether can be isolated from the rest. Practical Occultism, however, teaches how this can be done, and thus the tremendous force of etheric pressure can be brought into play.

Next, there is a vast store of potential energy which has become dormant in matter during the involution of the subtle into the gross, and by changing the condition of the matter some of this may be liberated and utilized, somewhat as latent energy in the form of heat may be liberated by a change in the condition of visible matter.

Fourthly, many striking results, both great and small, may be produced by an extension of a principle which may be described as that of sympathetic vibration.

Sympathetic Vibration: Illustrations taken from the physical plane seem generally to misrepresent rather than elucidate astral phenomena, because they can never be more than partially applicable; but the recollection of two simple facts of ordinary life may help to make this important branch of our subject clearer, if we are careful not to push the analogy further than it will hold good.

It is well known that if one of the wires of a harp be made to vibrate vigorously, its movement will call forth sympathetic vibrations in the corresponding strings of any number of harps placed round it, if they are tuned to exactly the same pitch.

It is also well known that when a large body of soldiers crosses a suspension bridge it is necessary for them to break step, since the perfect regularity of their ordinary march would set up a vibration in the bridge which would be intensified by every step they took, until the point of resistance of the iron was passed, when the whole structure would fly to pieces.

With these two analogies in our minds (never forgetting that they are only partial ones) it may seem more comprehensible that one who knows exactly at what rate to start his vibrations—knows, so to speak, the keynote of the class of matter he wishes to affect—should be able by sounding that keynote to call forth an immense number of sympathetic vibrations.

When this is done on the physical plane no additional energy is developed. But on the astral plane there is this difference: the matter with which we are dealing is far less inert, and so when called into action by these sympathetic vibrations it adds its own living force to the original impulse, which may thus be multiplied many-fold.

And then by further rhythmic repetition of the original impulse, as in the case of the soldiers marching over the bridge, the vibrations may be so intensified that the result is out of all apparent proportion to the cause. Indeed, it may be said that there is scarcely any limit to the conceivable achievements of this force in the hands of a great Adept who fully comprehends its possibilities, for the very building of the Universe itself was but the result of the vibrations set up by the Spoken Word.

Mantras: The class of mantras or spells which produce their result not by controlling some elemental, but merely by the repetition of certain sounds, also depend for their efficacy upon this action of sympathetic vibration.

Disintegration: The phenomenon of disintegration also may be brought about by the action of extremely rapid vibrations, which overcome the cohesion of the molecules of the object operated upon. A still higher rate of vibrations of a somewhat different type will separate these molecules into their constituent atoms. A body reduced by these means to the etheric condition can be moved by an astral current from one place to another with very great rapidity; and the moment that the force which has been exerted to put it into that condition is withdrawn. it will be forced by the etheric pressure to resume its original form.

It is in this way that objects are sometimes brought almost instantaneously from great distances at spiritualistic *séances,* and it is obvious that when disintegrated they could be passed with perfect ease through any solid substance, such, for example, as the wall of a house or the side of a locked box, so that what is commonly called "the passage of matter through matter" is seen, when properly understood, to be as simple as the passage of water through a sieve, or of a gas through a liquid in some chemical experiment.

Materialization: Since it is possible by an alteration of vibrations to change matter from the solid to the etheric condition, it will be comprehended that it is also possible to reverse the process and to bring etheric matter into the solid state.

As the one process explains the phenomenon of disintegration, so does the other that of materialization.

And just as in the former case a continued effort of will is necessary to prevent the object from resuming its original form, so in exactly the same way in the latter phenomenon a continued effort is necessary to prevent the materialized matter from relapsing into the etheric condition.

In the materializations seen at an ordinary *séance*, such matter as may be required is borrowed as far as possible from the medium's etheric double—an operation which is prejudicial to his health, and also undesirable in various other ways; and this explains the fact that the materialized form is usually strictly confined to the immediate neighborhood of the medium, and is subject to an attraction which is constantly drawing it back to the body from which it came, so that if kept away from the medium too long the figure collapses, and the matter which composed it, returning to the etheric condition, rushes back instantly to its source.

Why Darkness is required: The reason why the beings directing a *séance* find it easier to operate in darkness or in very subdued light will now be manifest, since their power would usually be insufficient to hold together a materialized form or even a "spirit hand" for more than a very few seconds amidst the intense vibrations set up by brilliant light.

The *habitués* of *séances* will no doubt have noticed that materializations are of three kinds. First, those which are tangible but not visible. Second, those which are visible but not tangible. And third, those which are both visible and tangible.

To the first kind, which is much the most common, belong the invisible spirit hands which so frequently stroke the faces of the sitters or carry small objects about the room, and the vocal organs from which the "direct voice" proceeds.

In this case, an order of matter is being used which can neither reflect nor obstruct light, but which is capable under certain conditions of setting up vibrations in the atmosphere which affect us as sound.

Spirit Photographs. A variation of this class is that kind of partial materialization which though incapable of reflecting any light that we can see, is yet able to affect some of the ultra-violet rays and can therefore make a more or less definite impression upon the camera, and so provide us with what are known as "spirit photographs."

**French illusionist Henry Robin poses
with a ghost in his 1863 photograph,
blending theatricality and early spirit
photography, as featured in The Perfect
Medium: Photography and the Occult
exhibit at the Metropolitan Museum of
Art (2005).**

When there is not sufficient power available to produce a perfect materialization we sometimes get the vaporous-looking form which constitutes our second class, and in such a case the "spirits" usually warn their sitters that the forms which appear must not be touched. In the rarer case of a full materialization there is sufficient power to hold together, at least for a few moments, a form which can be both seen and touched. When an Adept or pupil finds it necessary for any purpose to materialize his Mâyâvirûpa or his astral body, he does not draw upon either his own etheric double or anyone else's, since he has been taught how to extract the matter which he requires directly from the astral light or even from the Âkâsha.

Precipitation: We read a good deal in Theosophical literature about the precipitation of letters or pictures. This result, like everything else, may be obtained in several ways.

An Adept wishing to communicate with someone might place a sheet of paper before him, form an image of the writing which he wished to appear upon it, and draw from the astral light the matter wherewith to objectify that image.

Or if he preferred to do so it would be equally easy for him to produce the same result upon a sheet of paper lying before his correspondent, whatever might be the distance between them.

A third method which, since it saves time, is much more frequently adopted, is to impress the whole substance of the letter on the mind of some pupil and leave him to do the mechanical work of precipitation. That pupil would then take his sheet of paper, and, imagining he saw the letter written thereon in his Master's hand, would proceed to objectify the writing as before described.

If he found it difficult to perform simultaneously the two operations of drawing his material from the astral light and precipitating the writing on paper, he might have either ordinary ink or a small quantity of colored powder on the table beside him, which, being already physical matter, could be drawn upon more readily.

It is of course obvious that the possession of this power would be a very dangerous weapon in the hands of an unscrupulous person, since it is just as easy to imitate one man's handwriting as another's, and it would be impossible to detect by any ordinary means a forgery committed in this manner.

A pupil definitely connected with any Master has always an infallible test by which he knows whether any message really emanates from that Master or not, but for others the proof of its origin must always lie solely in the contents of the letter and the spirit breathing through it, as the handwriting, however cleverly imitated, is of absolutely no value as evidence.

As to speed, a pupil new to the work of precipitation would probably be able to image only a few words at a time, and would, therefore, get on hardly more rapidly than if he wrote his letter in the ordinary way, but a more experienced individual who could visualize a whole page or perhaps the entire letter at once would get through his work with greater facility. It is in this manner that quite long letters are sometimes produced in a few seconds at a *séance*.

When a picture must be precipitated, the method is precisely the same, except that here it is absolutely necessary that the entire scene should he visualized at once, and if many colors are required there is of course the additional complication of manufacturing them, keeping them separate, and reproducing accurately the exact tints of the scene to be represented.

Evidently there is scope here for the exercise of the artistic faculty, and it must not be supposed that every inhabitant of the astral plane could by this method produce an equally good picture; a man who had been a great artist in life, and had therefore learnt how to see and what to look for, would certainly be much more successful than the ordinary person if he attempted precipitation when on the astral plane after death.

Slate-writing: Slate-writing for the production of which under test conditions some of the greatest mediums have been so famous, is sometimes produced by precipitation. Though notably, it is more frequent that the fragment of pencil enclosed between the slates is guided by a spirit hand, of which only the tiny points sufficient to grasp it are materialized.

(Editor's Note: Henry Slade was probably the most prominent 19th century slate writer. But William Eglinton was equally acclaimed for his slate writings and materializations as was Dr. Monck, who combined slate writing with levitations and spirit apparitions. Jonathan Koons introduced an innovative "spirit room," creating a dedicated space for otherworldly communication.)

**The Eye of the Lord, Georgiana
Houghton (1870).**

Georgiana Houghton (1814–1884) was a 19th-century British artist, spiritualist, and medium known for her intricate, abstract watercolors and writings, which she called "spirit drawings." Guided by the spirits of angels, deceased family members, and Renaissance artists, Houghton created kaleidoscopic works that prefigured modern abstract art. Though she was not formally part of the Theosophical movement, Houghton was engaged with spiritualist movements of her time and shared commonalities with Theosophical interest in accessing unseen dimensions of existence and higher spiritual planes.

(Editor's note: *slate-writing* has influenced many artists and spiritual practitioners. Olga Worrall (1899–1991), a prominent Theosophist and medium, was known for her work with automatic writing; she also wrote several books, including *The Mediumship of Olga Worrall* (1977), where she discusses her mediumistic practices. Similarly, Geoffrey Hodson (1886–1983), a clairvoyant, involved in spiritual communication, authored *The Brotherhood of Angels and Men* (1944) and *The Spiritual Origins of Man* (1952), which reflect his Theosophical views. In visual art, Wassily Kandinsky's *Composition X* (1939), Kay Sage's *The Passage* (1956), and Yves Tanguy's *Indefinite Divisibility* (1942) both reflect mystical and subconscious processes, with Kandinsky's work exploring the spiritual and the abstract as influenced by his Theosophical beliefs.

The Surrealists, including André Breton (notably in his work *Nadja*, 1928), Salvador Dalí (whose *The Persistence of Memory* (1931) reflects the exploration of dreams and unconscious states), and Max Ernst (with works like *The Robing of the Bride* (1940)), all embraced automatic writing as a tool to access the unconscious. Today, artists like Julian Schnabel (*The Patients and the Doctors*, 1982) and Tracey Emin (*My Bed*, 1998) incorporate elements of spirituality and automatic process into their work, bringing the legacy of mystical explorations of the unconscious into contemporary literati conversation.)

Automatic writing on back of *The Eye of the Lord.*

Levitation: An occurrence which occasionally takes place at *séances*, and more frequently among eastern Yógîs, is what is called levitation—that is, the floating of a human body in the air. No doubt when this takes place in the case of a medium, he is often simply upborne by "spirit hands," but there is another and more scientific method of accomplishing this feat which is always used in the East, and occasionally here also.

Occult science is acquainted with a means of neutralizing or even entirely reversing the attraction of gravity, and it is obvious that by the judicious use of this power all the phenomena of levitation may be easily produced.

It was no doubt by a knowledge of this secret that some of the airships of ancient India and Atlantis were raised from the earth and made light enough to be readily moved and directed; and not improbably the same acquaintance with nature's finer forces greatly facilitated the labors of those who raised the enormous blocks of stone sometimes used in cyclopean architecture, or in the building of the Pyramids and Stonehenge.

Spirit Lights: With the knowledge of the forces of nature which the resources of the astral plane place at the command its inhabitants the production of what are called "spirit lights" is a very easy matter, whether they be of the mildly phosphorescent or the dazzling electrical variety, or those curious dancing globules of light into which a certain class of fire elementals so readily transform themselves. Since all light consists simply of vibrations of the ether, it is obvious that anyone who knows how to set up these vibrations can readily produce any kind of light that he wishes.

Handling Fire: It is by the aid of the etheric elemental essence also that the remarkable feat of handling fire unharmed is generally performed, though there are as usual other ways in which it can be done. The thinnest layer of etheric substance can be so manipulated as to be absolutely impervious to heat, and when the hand of a medium or sitter is covered with this, he may pick up burning coal or red-hot iron with perfect safety.

Transmutation: Most of the occurrences of the *séance*-room have now been referred to, but there are one or two of the rarer phenomena of the outer world which must not be left quite without mention in our list.

The transmutation of metals is commonly supposed to be a mere dream of the medieval alchemists, and no doubt in most cases the description of the phenomenon was merely a symbol of the purification of the soul; yet there seems to be some evidence that it was really accomplished by them on several occasions, and there are petty magicians in the East who profess to do it under test conditions even now. Be that as it may, it is evident that since the ultimate atom is one and the same in all substances, and it is only the methods of its combination that differ, anyone who possessed the power of reducing a piece of metal to the atomic condition and of re-arranging its atoms in some other form would have no difficulty in effecting transmutation to any extent that he wished.

Repercussion: The principle of sympathetic vibration mentioned above also provides the explanation of that strange and little-known phenomenon called repercussion by means of which any injury done to, or any mark made upon, the astral body in the course of its wanderings will be reproduced in the physical body.

We find traces of this in some of the evidence given at trials for witchcraft in the Middle Ages, in which it is not infrequently stated that some wound given to the witch when in the form of a dog or a wolf was found to have appeared in the corresponding part of her human body.

The same strange law has sometimes led to an entirely unjust accusation of fraud against a medium, because, for example, some coloring matter rubbed upon the hand of a materialized "spirit" was afterwards found upon his hand—the explanation being that in that case, as so often happens, the "spirit" was simply the medium's astral body or perhaps even his etheric double, forced by the guiding influences to take some form other than his own. In fact, the astral and physical bodies are so intimately connected that it is impossible to touch the keynote of one without immediately setting up exactly corresponding vibrations in the other.

6

CONCLUSION.

It is hoped that any reader who has been sufficiently interested to follow this treatise thus far, may by this time have a general idea of the astral plane and its possibilities, such as will enable him to understand and fit into their proper places in its scheme any facts in connection with it which he may pick up in his reading.

Though only the roughest sketch has been given of a very great subject, enough has perhaps been said to show the extreme importance of astral perception in the study of biology, physics, chemistry, astronomy, medicine and history, and the great impulse which might be given by its development to all these sciences. Yet its attainment should never be regarded as an end in itself, since any means adopted with that object in view would inevitably lead to what is called in the East the *laukika* method of development—a system by which certain psychic powers are indeed acquired, but only for the present personality; and since their acquisition is surrounded by no safeguards, the student is extremely likely to misuse them. To this class belong all systems which involve the use of drugs, invocation of elementals, or the practices of Hatha Yoga.

The other method, which is called the *lokottara*, consists of Raj Yoga or spiritual progress, and though it may be somewhat slower than the other, whatever is acquired along this line is gained for the permanent individuality, and never lost again, while the guiding care of a Master ensures perfect safety from misuse of power as long as his orders are scrupulously obeyed.

The opening of astral vision must be regarded then only as a stage in the development of something infinitely nobler—merely as a step, and a very small step, on that great Upward Path which leads men to the sublime heights of Adeptship, and beyond even that through glorious vistas of wisdom and power such as our finite minds cannot now conceive.

Yet let no one think it an unmixed blessing to have the wider sight of the astral plane, for upon one in whom that vision is opened the sorrow and misery, the evil and the greed of the world press as an everpresent burden, until he often feels inclined to echo the passionate adjuration of Schiller: "Why hast thou cast me thus into the town of the ever-blind, to proclaim thine oracle with the opened sense? Take back this sad clear-sightedness; take from mine eyes this cruel light! Give me back my blindness—the happy darkness of my senses; take back thy dreadful gift!" This feeling is perhaps not an unnatural one in the earlier stages of the Path, yet higher sight and deeper knowledge soon bring to the student the perfect certainty that all things are working together for the eventual good of all—that

> Hour after hour, like an opening flower,
> Shall truth after truth expand.
> For the sun may pale, and the stars may fail,
> But the Law of Good shall stand.
> Its splendor glows and its influence grows
> As Nature's slow work appears,
> From the zoophyte small to the Lords of all,
> Through kalpas and scrores of years.

References

*

Atwater, P. M. H. *The Big Book of Near-Death Experiences: The Ultimate Guide to What Happens After We Die.* Rainbow Ridge Publishing, 2007.

Bailey, Alice A. *The Externalisation of the Hierarchy.* Lucis Publishing, 1957.

Benjamin, Walter. "The Work of Art in the Age of Mechanical Reproduction." *Illuminations*, ed. by Hannah Arendt, translated by Harry Zohn, Schocken Books, 1968, pp. 217–251.

*Besant, Annie and C.W. Leadbeater. *Thought-Forms: Theosophy for the 21st Century.* Decatur Dixon Press, 2024.

Besant, Annie. *Death—and After?* Theosophical Publishing Society, 1893.

Blavatsky, Helena Petrovna. *The Secret Doctrine: The Synthesis of Science, Religion, and Philosophy.* Theosophical Publishing House, 1888.

Braude, Stephen E. *The Limits of Influence: Psychokinesis, the Inexplicable, and the Skeptic's Struggle.* Routledge & Kegan Paul. 1986

Buhlman, William. *Adventures Beyond the Body: How to Experience Out-of-Body Travel.* Hampton Roads, 2001.

Cannon, Dolores. *The Convoluted Universe* (Vols. 1-5). Ozark Mountain Publishing, 2001–2011.

Castaneda, Carlos. *A Separate Reality: Further Conversations with Don Juan.* Simon & Schuster, 1971.

Castaneda, Carlos. *The Art of Dreaming.* Harper Collins, 1993.

Castaneda, Carlos. *The Teachings of Don Juan: A Yaqui Way of Knowledge.* University of California Press, 1968.

Corbell, J. (2020). *The Phenomenon: The Disclosure of the UFOs.* Directed by Jeremy Corbell.

Corso, Philip J., and William J. Birnes. *The Day After Roswell.* Pocket Books, 1997.

Davis, Wade. *One River: Explorations and Discoveries in the Amazon Rainforest*. Simon & Schuster, 1996.

Davis, Wade. *The Serpent and the Rainbow*. Simon & Schuster, 1985.

Davis, Wade. *The Wayfinders: Why Ancient Wisdom Matters in the Modern World*. House of Anansi Press, 2018.

Dewan, William J. "'A Saucerful of Secrets': An Interdisciplinary Analysis of UFO Experiences." *The Journal of American Folklore*, vol. 119, no. 472, 2006, pp. 184–202.

Doyle, Arthur Conan. *The History of Spiritualism*. Cassell, 1926.

Eliade, Mircea. *Shamanism: Archaic Techniques of Ecstasy*. Princeton University Press, 1951. (English translation, 1964).

Elizondo, Luis. *Imminent: Inside the Pentagon's Hunt for UFOs*. William Morrow, 2024.

Emerson, Ralph Waldo. *Essays, The Over Soul*. United States, J. Munroe, 1841.

Ford, T. *Altered States and Modern Society: A New Perspective*. Oxford University Press, 2019

Foucault, Michel. *Discipline and Punish: The Birth of the Prison*. Translated by Alan Sheridan, Vintage Books, 1977.

Greer, Steven. (2001). *Disclosure: Military and Government Witnesses Reveal the Greatest Secrets in Modern History*. Crossroad Press.

Griffiths, Roland R., et al. "Psilocybin-Occasioned Mystical-Type Experience: Immediate and Persisting Dose-Related Effects." *Psychopharmacology*, vol. 218, no. 4, 2011, pp. 649–665.

Grof, Stanislav. *The Holotropic Mind: The Three Levels of Human Consciousness and How They Shape Our Lives*. Harper Collins, 1992.

Grof, Stanislav. *The Way of the Psychonaut: Stanislav Grof's Journey of Consciousness*. The Stanislav Grof Foundation, 2020.

Grof, Stanislav. *Transpersonal Psychology: A Postmodern View*. SUNY Press, 1998.

Harner, Michael. *The Way of the Shaman*. Harper & Row, 1980.

Hodson, Geoffrey. *The Brotherhood of Angels and of Men*. The Theosophical Publishing House, 1946.

Houdini, Harry. *A Magician Among the Spirits*. Harper & Brothers, 1924.

Hynek, J. Allen. *The UFO Experience: A Scientific Inquiry*. Henle Communications, 1972.

Jacobs, David M. *Secret Life: Firsthand Accounts of UFO Abductions*. Simon & Schuster, 1992.

James, William. *The Varieties of Religious Experience*. Longmans, Green, 1902.

Kalweit, Holger. *Dreamtime and Inner Space: The World of the Shaman*. Shambhala. 1988.

Kardec, Allan. *Le Livre des Esprits (The Spirits' Book)*. Didier et Cie, 1857.

Kean, Leslie (2020). *UFOs: Generals, Pilots, and Government Officials Go on the Record*. St. Martin's Press.

Leadbeater, C.W. *The Masters and the Path*. The Theosophical Publishing House, 1925.

Leadbeater, C.W., and Annie Besant. *Thought-Forms*. Decatur Dixon Press, 2024.

Mack, John E. *Abduction: Human Encounters with Aliens*. Scribner, 1994.

Macpherson, James, and Hugh Blair. *The poems of Ossian*. New York, E. Kearny, 1846.

Monroe, Robert. *Journeys Out of the Body*. Doubleday, 1971.

Narby, Jeremy. *The Cosmic Serpent: DNA and the Origins of Knowledge*. Tarcher, 1999.

Pollan, Michael. *How to Change Your Mind: What the New Science of Psychedelics Teaches Us About Consciousness, Dying, Addiction, Depression, and Transcendence*. Penguin Press, 2018.

Pope, Nick. (2018). *Open Skies, Closed Minds*. Watkins Publishing.

Presti, David, and B. Alan Wallace. *Mind Beyond Brain: Buddhism, Science, and the Paranormal*. Columbia University Press, 2018.

Radin, Dean. *Entangled Minds: Extrasensory Experiences in a Quantum Reality*. Paraview Pocket Books, 2006.

Scott, Sir Walter. *The Highland Widow*. Hesperus Press, 2010 (1830).

Sheldrake, Merlin. *Entangled Life: How Fungi Make Our Worlds, Change Our Minds & Shape Our Futures*. Random House, 2020

Sheldrake, Rupert. *A New Science of Life: The Hypothesis of Morphic Resonance*. Park Street Press, 1981.

Sheldrake, Rupert. *The Sense of Being Stared At: And Other Aspects of the Extended Mind*. Random House, 2003.

Steiner, Rudolf. *The Philosophy of Freedom: A Modern Introduction to the Philosophy of Spiritual Activity*. Anthroposophic Press, 1995.

Stephen, Michelle. *Asia's Gifts: A Study of the Mekeo People of Papua New Guinea*. University of Hawaii Press, 1998.

Tedlock, Barbara. *The Woman in the Shaman's Body: Reclaiming the Feminine in Religion and Medicine*. Bantam Books, 2005.

Thurman, Robert A. F., translator. *The Tibetan Book of the Dead*. Bantam Books, 1994.

Tumin, Remy. "Did Aliens Land on Earth in 1945? A Defense Bill Seeks Answers." *The New York Times*, 13 Jan. 2023, https://www.nytimes.com/2023/01/13/us/ufo-new-mexico-congress.html?smid=url-share.

Wilcock, David. *The Source Field Investigations: The Hidden Science and Lost Civilizations Behind the 2012 Prophecies*. Dutton, 2011.

Yingling, M. E., Yingling, C. W., and B. A. Bell. "Faculty Perceptions of Unidentified Aerial Phenomena." *Humanities and Social Sciences Communications*, vol. 10, no. 246, 2023.

Charles Webster Leadbeater
(1854–1934)

Your Astral Journey

Now that you have read Leadbeater's account, looked at some of the artwork coming out of the Theosophical movement, and skimmed some of the literature on this subject, you may be wondering how you might experiment with this.

As we have learned, astral projection is the practice of separating your consciousness from your physical body to explore a non-physical, non-linear plane of existence. Unlike lucid dreaming, which involves becoming aware of and potentially controlling your dream environment, astral projection is a conscious effort to leave the physical body and navigate an external, non-mental realm.

To begin astral projecting, find a quiet, comfortable space where you won't be disturbed. Relax your body and mind through deep breathing or progressive muscle relaxation techniques. Set a clear intention for the practice, focusing your mind on the goal of astral projection to minimize doubt or fear. Once relaxed, lie down comfortably, close your eyes, and enter a deeply calm state, balancing on the edge of sleep while remaining consciously aware.

As you approach this hypnagogic state, you may notice vibrations or sensations that many practitioners describe as a precursor to separation. Focus on that! Allow these vibrations to intensify without letting them overwhelm you. Visualize yourself leaving your body, either by floating upward or rolling out of it. Concentrate on the sensation of movement, as though a part of you is gently detaching. If separation occurs, remain calm and observe your surroundings without overthinking or becoming overly excited, as these responses can interrupt the experience.

During the astral journey, you may explore the non-physical realm while keeping the intention of returning to your physical body. When you are ready to end your experience, visualize re-entering your body and slowly, calmly, transition back to full consciousness.

Astral projection differs significantly from lucid dreaming. Lucid dreaming happens within the mind's dream state, where the dreamer becomes aware they are dreaming and can manipulate the dream environment. Astral projection, on the other hand, involves navigating external planes while maintaining conscious awareness.

It is important to note that astral projection is a subjective practice, and experiences vary greatly among individuals. Approach this practice with an open but critical mind. If you experience anxiety, fear, or difficulty distinguishing between physical and non-physical realities, consult an expert. Always ensure you are in a safe, secure environment before attempting astral projection. Finally, enjoy the experience. Whether you reach a full separation or simply achieve a deeper state of relaxation and awareness, this is an opportunity for growth and exploration.

Above all else, be kind to yourself, be kind to others, and allow the benevolent astral beings to love you.

About the DDP Press

Please visit us at
DecaturDixonPress.com

The Decatur Dixon Press is the first publishing company to double as a work of experimental art. Founded by a visual anthropologist and an art historian-curator, DDP seeks wholly interdisciplinary content that rethinks what is possible, even challenging traditional book organization and structure. Its curated series of illustrated favorites explores the afterlife of the writer, the artist, the artwork, and even the book itself as a material artifact, giving each a second chance to speak to us once more.

We hope you will enjoy additional titles in the illustrated classics series.

Pierre and Jean: an illustrated classic. Guy de Maupassant

R.U.R. (Rossum's Universal Robots): A Fantastic Melodrama in Three Acts and an Epilogue. Karel Čapek

Chess, an illustrated novella. Stefan Zweig

Pan. Knut Hamsun

Bartleby, the Scrivener. Herman Melville

Thought-Forms. Annie Besant and C.W. Leadbeater

Swift Poetry. Curated and illustrated by Lula Crowder

Decatur Dixon is widely read and widely traveled. While he has sampled every dish and libation placed in front of him, and hunts or fishes at least once a week, his favorite activity is reading—every genre, every era. This book is among his many favorites.

www.ingramcontent.com/pod-product-compliance
Lightning Source LLC
Chambersburg PA
CBHW020358130626
46549CB00006B/2340